The Beatitudes

The Beatitudes

Jesus' Formula for Happiness

Rubel Shelly

20th Century Christian
2809 Granny White Pike
Nashville, Tennessee 37204

Other Books by Rubel Shelly

Going On To Maturity
Young People and Their Lord
A Book-By-Book Study of the Old Testament
A Book-by-Book Study of the New Testament
Living By The Rules
The (Im)Perfect Church
What Christian Living Is All About
Something to Hold Onto
The Lamb and His Enemies
Of Human Origins
I Just Want to Be a Christian

Booklets
Do You Ever Have Doubts?
If I Didn't Believe the Bible
Marriage, Divorce, and Reconciliation
Would You Kick a Blind Man?
God's Grace
Life's Priorities
You Can Start Over
Growing Older
Keys to Effective Parenting
Marriage Traps
We Have Met the Enemy
Christians Only

Copyright © 1982, 1984 by Rubel Shelly
Nashville, Tennessee
ISBN 0-89098-473-5

To

J. D. St Clair

brother, friend, encourager

Table of Contents

Introduction

In 1776 the Founding Fathers of the United States of America proclaimed the pursuit of happiness to be an "unalienable right" of humankind. Since that declaration, it seems to have been taken for granted that happiness is a God-given, inseparable part of the American destiny.

There have always been people ready to capitalize on this desire for happiness by selling gullible folk their particular dream or product. Various utopian movements were spawned in the early days of America; books promising to show the path to personal happiness and fulfillment sell millions of copies every year; automobiles, deodorants, and toothpastes are sold with the promise of happiness to their users.

But in an era of affluence and increased leisure, people seem to be finding that happiness is ever more elusive. We have money, live in nice houses, travel as we choose, educate ourselves and our children, and spend billions on recreation. Yet the best of times seems to many people to be the worst of times.

The wealth and technology which were expected to

make people happy have created new problems. While showering us with an abundance of goods, they have also brought massive air and water pollution, power blackouts, traffic congestion, and devastating cycles of inflation and recession.

The suicide rate among young people has risen sharply during the last couple of decades. It has been estimated that probably ten million persons in the United States need professional treatment for depression.

We humans seem to expect happiness, but we do not know where or how to find it. Like Solomon, we look everywhere on earth for happiness and come away saying, "All is vanity and a striving after wind" (Ecclesiastes 1:14).

Human beings can neither create nor find happiness through our own unaided efforts. Happiness is a *gift from God.*

Happiness is being a child of God. And although uninformed people sometimes speak of the "Universal Fatherhood of God" and imply that everyone is a child of God, it just isn't so. Jesus once said to a group of people, "You are of your father the devil" (John 8:44a).

No one is a child of God until he or she has been born anew. And the person who has been reborn into the family of God will live so as to honor his or her father.

Yes, it is happiness to know you are a child of God. It is happiness to know that he loves you with all the love of his great heart. It is happiness to know that you can always call on him, to know that he is ready to hear you, to know that he is eager to pour his best blessings upon you. It is happiness to know he loves you more tenderly than any earthly father can love his child.

There is so much misery in human hearts today that suicide is now acknowledged to be among the top ten causes of death among adults in this country. Perhaps the saddest thing about all this misery is its unnecessary nature. The two paths of happiness and misery lie before each one of us, and each makes his own choice of the road he will travel. You *can* be happy, if you *choose* to be.

As the great lawgiver and statesman Moses approached

his death, he assembled the people he loved for a final time. He spoke to the Israelites about the blessings that would come to them from obedience to God and warned of the horrors that would consume them if they were disobedient. Here are the closing words of his moving exhortation: "I call heaven and earth to witness against you this day, that I have set before you life and death, blessing and curse; therefore *choose life, that you and your descendants may live, loving the Lord your God, obeying his voice, and cleaving to him; for that means life to you and length of days ...*" (Deuteronomy 30:19-20a).

God has put it within the power of every human being to choose a destiny. Your fate is not forced upon you; you choose what your life will be. You will not be happy or unhappy due to some genetic accident; you will *choose* joy or sorrow.

You choose happiness as you believe in and obey Jesus. You condemn yourself to unhappiness by turning from him and his will.

This book is designed to explore the meaning of the happiness discussed in the Bible. In particular, it addresses this important subject through a study of Jesus' prescription for human blessedness in the Beatitudes.

I hope the study ahead will be meaningful to you. I hope it will enable you to come away from the opening verses of the Sermon on the Mount with firm confidence that you know where to go for the happiness you seek.

Rubel Shelly

1/ Happiness is Such a Rare Thing

"How may I be happy?" is the question of every human being. Each of us is striving constantly to attain a state of life and condition of mind that can be termed *happy*. It has ever been and always will be this way.

Solomon related his attempts at finding happiness in the Book of Ecclesiastes. He wrote: "I searched with my mind how to cheer my body with wine – my mind still guiding me with wisdom – and how to lay hold on folly, till I might see what was good for the sons of men to do under heaven during the few days of their life. I made great works; I built houses and planted vineyards for myself; I made myself gardens and parks, and planted in them all kinds of fruit trees. I made myself pools from which to water the forest of growing trees. I bought male and female slaves ... I had also great possessions of herds and flocks ... I also gathered for myself silver and gold ... I got singers ..." (2:3-8).

The world's teeming millions today are searching in the same places Solomon did in their efforts to find personal happiness. They try achievement, fame, wealth, entertainment, wine, and the like. And more and more of them are being forced to the same sad conclusion Solomon reached: "I have seen everything that is done under the sun; and behold, all is vanity and a striving after wind" (1:14).

Is the Search Sinful?

Is it wrong to want to be happy? Is it mere selfishness on our part? Would it therefore be wrong to seek God's blessing for our search for personal happiness? Not at all.

The Bible makes it clear that God wants his creatures to be happy. Not only that, but he wants to provide the happiness for which we search instinctively. "Happy the people to whom such blessings fall! Happy the people whose God is the Lord!" (Psalm 144:15). "Happy is he whose help is the God of Jacob, whose hope is in the Lord his God" (Psalm 146:5). "He who gives heed to the word will prosper, and happy is he who trusts in the Lord" (Proverbs 16:20). "Rejoice in the Lord always; again I will say, Rejoice" (Philippians 4:4).

But is this spirit of Christian joy, blessedness, and peace of mind the spirit of our age? Indeed not! Despair and meaninglessness seem to characterize our world. Whole hosts of people would echo Dostoevsky's lament over the "tears of humanity with which the earth is soaked from its crust to its center." Pessimism and the flight from reality are common denominators for too many people of our day.

The Futility of Life Without God

Why does a middle-aged woman spend her day in bed sedated by drugs or sitting in a darkened house drinking endlessly? Why does a reasonably successful businessman have a clandestine affair with his young secretary? Why does a bright, sensitive, and attractive teen-aged girl run away from home? Why are so many people – both young and old – turning to the mystical religions of the East or the cultic forms of western religion?

Why? *Life has ceased to have any real meaning for these people.*

Religion has lost its place of significance in the lives of people generally. Many "religious" people no longer believe that Jesus was actually born of a virgin, yet they go through the form of participation in religious services. What meaning can it have? People who hold membership in religious groups in America live amorally and on a level with the world. Why? Life has lost its meaning for these people. It has become a boring exercise in futility.

Paul E. Johnson has commented on the social alienation of modern times and observes: "In our time we have been uprooted from our former homeland, adrift in a mobile and changing society. We are lonely in crowds who seem not to care, pushed to and fro by machines to serve and be served, until we too become mechanical and act like machines. We meet the other persons as strangers, but mostly by external contacts passing by or bouncing away as if we were rubber balls. We are hollow men who do not know the inner life of outer persons, and so we give attention mainly to the external appearance. Estranged from them or used by them, we are empty within ourselves, lost souls for whom no one seems to care." [*Christian Advocate*, Sept. 23, 1964, p. 7].

The Happiness We Seek

More and more of us are recognizing that happiness cannot be found in the places where it has been sought most frequently.

Happiness has been thought to consist of a bank account in excess of a certain figure, life in a particular neighborhood where the houses are all of a certain price range, a job with positive security and opportunities for advancement, freedom to participate in popular sports and social activities, lots of paid vacation time, etc. But we are beginning to see the light. We are being honest enough with ourselves to admit that happiness is a *quality of spirit* rather than a circumstance created by the right combination of gadgets, bucks, and glamor.

The periodic upheavals among idealistic and sensitive young people in our midst is eloquent testimony to the superficiality of the allegedly stable and happy world built by their elders. The children have seen the misery of spirit which grips their parents in the midst of the trappings of affluence. They see the materialism, greed, and hypocrisy which surround them and are repulsed. Then, as they reflect on the situation, their revulsion becomes either blind fury or passive disenchantment. Thus some act violently with a view toward overthrowing "the establishment" and others turn to drugs and promiscuity just to get the whole depressing issue off their minds.

It has been interesting to watch the evolution of thought among the young people who were the rebels or dropouts of the '60s and '70s. They didn't find fulfillment in their adopted lifestyles and have come back toward the establishment they once disdained. They finally had to admit that their method was as shallow and inadequate as the one they were protesting. Happiness did not come from dropping out of or striking out at society.

Jesus announced the secret to true and lasting happiness in the Beatitudes. *The Beatitudes are statements of the basic attitudes which are necessary in order for one to be accepted by God and to live the Christian life successfully.*

Jesus constantly emphasized that human lives can be happy only when human hearts are right. In the Beatitudes he pointed to the right qualities of heart upon which successful living depends.

"Seeing the crowds, he went up on the mountain, and when he sat down his disciples came to him. And he opened his mouth and taught them, saying:

"Blessed are the poor in spirit, for theirs is the kingdom of heaven.

"Blessed are those who mourn, for they shall be comforted.

"Blessed are the meek, for they shall inherit the earth.

"Blessed are those who hunger and thirst for righteousness, for they shall be satisfied.

"Blessed are the merciful, for they shall obtain mercy.

"Blessed are the pure in heart, for they shall see God.

"Blessed are the peacemakers, for they shall be called sons of God.

"Blessed are those who are persecuted for righteousness' sake, for theirs is the kingdom of heaven.

"Blessed are you when men shall revile you and persecute you and utter all kinds of evil against you falsely on my account. Rejoice and be glad, for your reward is great in heaven, for so men persecuted the prophets who were before you."

(Matthew 5:1-12).

Please observe that each of these statements begins with the word "blessed." With the passing of time, the meaning of this word has become obscure to most of us. It has come to have a sort of sanctimonious flavor. It is even thought of as a sort of technical word for use in theology.

In an effort to avoid this false impression concerning the word "blessed," several modern translations use the word "happy" in these verses. This is the word used for this series of studies – as indicated by the various chapter titles in the book: "Happiness is Humility," "Happiness is Mourning," etc. In using this word, however, we must keep in mind that a particular type of happiness is intended. Genuine and lasting happiness is what Jesus offers, as opposed to the fleeting and often deceptive pleasures of sin.

The word "blessed" or "happy" is translated from a Greek word (*makarios*) which was used originally to describe the state of the gods as opposed to that of mere mortals. The Greeks also used a form of the same word to refer to Cyprus (*he makaria*), "the Happy Isle." They believed Cyprus to be so lovely and fertile a place that a man could find happiness enough there so he would never want to leave it.

5

In the New Testament, this word was used by Spirit-guided writers to refer to the state of spiritual and moral prosperity which people could share in Christ. It was used to point to the highest happiness human creatures can enjoy in this world.

Unlike the purely human forms of happiness men and women struggle to gain in the pursuit of power, sensual pleasure, and wealth, this spiritual happiness cannot be taken away from its possessor. It is untouchable by the changing conditions of the world. The failure of one's health, the collapse of an important plan, the disappointment of a cherished ambition, or so trivial a thing as a change in the weather can spoil the joys this world can give. The believer has an unassailable happiness which comes of walking in the light of God's presence; this joy can never be denied by the changing fortunes of the world.

An Important Clarification

A word of caution and explanation may be needed at this point. As we begin studying the Lord's prescription for human happiness, it is important that we not confuse that holy plan with some of its popular counterfeits.

True religion is intended to be a process of reconciliation by means of which God's human offspring are restored to fellowship with himself. It is a thoroughly spiritual exercise which results in eternal life. It is not mere auto-suggestion and thinly veiled psychotherapy designed to help people in their personal and professional lives.

A vast amount of positive-thinking literature has been produced in the past few years which offers nothing more than this sort of materialistic approach to religion. For example, one of the best-selling of those books counsels its readers to go to the mirror in the morning, look themselves in the eye, and say aloud three times "I believe, I believe, I believe!" But believe WHAT? Or, better yet, believe WHOM?

The Beatitudes are not to be confused with that sort of approach to religion.

The Christian religion is not a crutch for humanity's

lame spirit. Neither is God the brand name for a tranquilizer or spiritual aspirin. And those who can see no more to the divine offer of eternal life than an effort to "bring out the best in each of us" are worshiping the creature rather than the Creator.

The "happiness" offered by the Beatitudes is far more than the superficial gaity of worldly life or the light-hearted frame of mind which some religious teachers and writers seem to see as the essence of true religion. It is a spiritual quality of inner joy which the world cannot take from the child of God. It is the state which was characteristic of Jesus Christ himself. He possessed the character which is defined by these statements and was able – even in the midst of personal sorrows, rejection, and humiliation – to find inner peace and happiness.

One author has put it this way: "The word 'blessed' as used by Jesus in the introduction of each of the beatitudes means far more than we usually mean by it. We can best illustrate it. We are out on the ocean in one of our large ships during the raging of a storm. The waves are rolling high and everything on the surface of the water is disturbed and even the vessel is rocking back to and fro like a drunken man. But if we could go to the bottom of the ocean we would find perfect calmness – nothing is disturbed – nothing is being moved. That is the condition of the soul in the meaning of the word 'blessed' as used by Jesus in the beatitudes." [Harvey Scott, *The Sermon on the Mount*, p. 15].

The Source of Happiness

We could not have known what true happiness is without a revelation from God. Our thinking tends to become confused because of sin.

One who was himself everything a person ought to be came and showed us the character and manner of life which is truly happy and then told us how to share it. No one can follow his code of conduct who is not in him and strengthened by him.

The gospel of Christ is concerned with the proclamation

of salvation through him who has died in our place. It is not a mere series of aphorisms or moral exhortations which will be recognized by wise men and women. It is the power of God unto salvation (Romans 1:16).

Happiness results from standing in right relationship with God and neighbor. And only those who are poor in spirit, meek, hungry and thirsty for righteousness, merciful, pure in heart, peacemakers, and willing to suffer for what is right are capable of living in this right relationship. So the study of these Beatitudes is a must rather than an option for anyone who would live the truly happy life.

One other point needs to be made about the Christlike character involved in the Beatitudes. This blessedness is not to be developed in some ideal world under ideal circumstances but right where we live today.

In a world filled with sin, suffering, and sorrows, God wants to demonstrate through his children that these traits of spiritual life can be developed and maintained. Happiness opens out before those who choose this path.

Conclusion

As we study each of the Beatitudes in its turn, each of us will be impressed anew with the Lord's ability to compress so much truth into such brief statements. We will say, as the people of his own time, "No man ever spoke like this man!" (John 7:46).

Questions for Discussion

1. Examine the Book of Ecclesiastes to determine the different things Solomon experimented with in his effort to be happy. What conclusion did he reach in the last chapter?
2. Do you agree that "life has lost its meaning" for most people of our time? Defend your answer.
3. What are the principal things people associate with happiness today?
4. Is it a legitimate expectation of Christianity that people should be happy who follow Jesus?

5. Discuss the statement: "The Beatitudes are statements of the basic attitudes which are necessary in order for one to be accepted by God and to live the Christian life successfully."
6. Contrast what the lesson called "real happiness" and "artificial happiness." Consider, for example, the lifestyle of some of the world's celebrities which has (by their own admission) left them with a feeling of emptiness and even driven some to suicide.
7. Do Christians ever seek happiness in the wrong places? What accounts for this sort of mistake?
8. Does one have to be in ideal circumstances in order to be happy? Cf. Acts 16:25.
9. Some religious literature interprets Christianity only in terms of its present value in changing society or improving one's personal state. Contrast this with the biblical view.
10. Can you think of someone who would benefit from studying these lessons? Will you invite him/her to class next week?

2/ Happiness is Humility

There is something immediately startling about each of the Beatitudes, for the traits of character praised in them are not the ones generally prized by men of our day or exhibited by them. Nowhere is this any more apparent than with the very first Beatitude. *"Blessed are the poor in spirit, for theirs is the kingdom of heaven"* (Matthew 5:3). *Happiness is to be found in being poor?* Preposterous! Surely this is a self-contradictory statement. We are accustomed to think that people who are poor must be unhappy. But Jesus plainly says that *happiness* is to be found through *poverty.* But wait. Perhaps we have not looked closely enough at his statement to see its real meaning.

When we use the words "poor" or "poverty," our minds usually apply them to material things. We think immediately of people who have very little of this world's goods. Is that what Jesus was saying? Is there some inherent spiritual virtue in being poor and in need of life's physical necessities?

Some Helpful Clarifications

There is no necessary blessing or curse in either material prosperity or poverty. The Lord's good friend at Bethany, Lazarus, appears to have been a rather prosperous man who feared God and shared the companionship of the Lord. On the other hand, there is a second man in the Gospels whose name was also Lazarus but who was very poor. He was a beggar who had been afflicted with a disease which produced loathsome sores. But his poverty did not cause him to be estranged from God. When he died, he was carried by angels into the bosom of Abraham (Luke 16:19-31).

Thus the Bible tells of two men by the same name who were poles apart in terms of social standing and economic status. Wealth did not keep the one from being saved; poverty did not keep the other from heaven.

Now surely there is a danger in being rich. One may pursue his wealth to the neglect of the true God. He may put his trust in money. Paul warns us: "But those who desire to be rich fall into temptation, into a snare, into many senseless and hurtful desires that plunge men into ruin and destruction" (1 Timothy 6:9). The Lord himself urged people to put primary emphasis on laying up treasures in heaven rather than on earth (Matthew 6:19-21).

But surely there is also a danger in poverty. An individual in terribly destitute circumstances may assume that God has forsaken him and turn away from God in bitterness. Or he may take matters into his own hands and steal in order to get the things he needs.

Knowing the threat of both wealth and poverty to one's spiritual life, the author of Proverbs 30:8-9 prayed: "Give me neither poverty nor riches; feed me with the food that is needful for me, lest I be full, and deny thee, and say, 'Who is the Lord?' or lest I be poor, and steal, and profane the name of my God."

Jesus was not speaking of material poverty in this Beatitude. Therefore, though it is true that many valuable lessons could be gained from a consideration of how to deal with deprivation and poverty in physical things, such things would be inappropriate to the understanding of the Beatitude at hand. Jesus is talking about those who are poor *in spirit.*

Again, however, we should be warned against drawing too hasty a conclusion. Perhaps there are too many people who think of the person who is "poor in spirit" as the poor-spirited, dejected, self-pitying soul who gives way when he ought to resist, who regards the battle as lost before the fight has really even begun, who lacks persistence, moral courage, and resoluteness. These are serious defects in human character and would not be commended by the Lord. As you will see shortly, the type of character the Lord sets before us in this Beatitude is certainly not of this distasteful sort.

Who Are the Poor in Spirit?

Who, then, are the poor in spirit? In his little book on the Beatitudes, John Redhead has made this very helpful suggestion: "We can get closer to our Lord's meaning if we substitute for the word 'spirit' our more modern word 'ego.' Ego means self, and to be rich in ego is to have too much of the same. We know people who are rich in ego, and we do not like them. They are proud and haughty and conceited. They have an overweening sense of their own importance. Those who are rich in ego are the self-satisfied, the self-sufficient, the self-seeking, and the self-centered. Says a contemporary novelist about one of her characters: 'Edith was a little country bounded on the north, south, east and west by Edith.' To be rich in ego is to be self-contained. It is to possess an acute awareness that one's world begins and ends with self." [*Finding Meaning in the Beatitudes*, p. 12].

Being poor in spirit is simply being the opposite of everything that is summed up in the word "proud." Blessed is the man who is *not* proud, for the heart that is filled with self has no room for God. The man who believes he is the master of his own fate and has need of nothing

13

beyond himself will never even seek God. Only the man who has been emptied of his arrogance can be saved.

The "wealthy in spirit" are sure they can get along quite well without God. They have no desire to hear and no inclination to obey the gospel. They certainly do not intend to deny themselves anything in order to follow Christ.

To be "poor in spirit" is to see ourselves as we really are – lost sinners. It is to be aware of how desperately we need the grace of God. In fact, one modern translation of this Beatitude renders it: "Blessed are those who feel their spiritual need."

If you would see the contrast between pride and humility in bold relief, take note of this parable of our Lord: "He also told this parable to some who trusted in themselves that they were righteous and despised others: 'Two men went up into the temple to pray, one a Pharisee and the other a tax collector. The Pharisee stood and prayed thus with himself, "God, I thank thee that I am not like other men, extortioners, unjust, adulterers, or even like this tax collector. I fast twice a week, I give tithes of all that I get." But the tax collector, standing far off, would not even lift up his eyes to heaven, but beat his breast, saying, "God, be merciful to me a sinner!" I tell you, this man went down to his house justified rather than the other; for every one who exalts himself will be humbled, but he who humbles himself will be exalted' " (Luke 18:9-14).

The Pharisee was rich in spirit. He was self-righteous, conceited, and proud of his spiritual purity and good works. But heaven refused this man precisely because of his pride. The tax collector, poor in spirit because he saw himself as he really was before God, was accepted in his humility. What a warning there is in this story for us.

Too many people are talking of their good lives and good works as if they were expecting salvation as a debt owed them by God. How absurd! Human beings can make no claims upon God. Salvation is a gift, a *free* gift. Any person who does not feel and freely admit his or her spiritual need will not come to receive it.

Until pride has been overcome in an individual's life,

there is no hope of attaining the state of happiness for which we long. There is no hope of entering the spiritual blessedness which God gives his own. Only when a penitent soul possesses the humility and sense of spiritual need necessary to make him cast aside his own righteousness and submit totally to the will of God can he be saved. There is an old hymn which expresses all this very succinctly:

> Nothing in my hand I bring;
> simply to thy cross I cling;
> Naked come to thee for dress;
> helpless, look to thee for grace.
> Foul, I to the fountain fly;
> wash me, Savior, or I die.

How This Spirit is Manifested

The individual who is truly poor in spirit is the one who readily accepts the truthfulness of Christ's statement: "Apart from me you can do nothing" (John 15:5). He has ceased putting his trust in the wisdom of this world and has put his complete dependence in divine wisdom. He has seen the futility of striving for the acclaim of the world and has devoted himself to the humble service of God. He has learned that "God opposes the proud, but gives grace to the humble" (James 4:6). He has given up his resistance to the will of God and is submitting himself daily to the divine will.

Think how this spirit is manifested in a practical way in the life of (1) an alien sinner desiring salvation from his or her sins, (2) a Christian who is attempting to grow in the grace and knowledge of the Lord Jesus Christ, and (3) a church.

First, it is essential that one be poor in spirit in order to be saved from sin.

Pride makes people unwilling to face the fact that they are lost in sin and in desperate need of salvation. It also makes us unwilling to accept the fact that we cannot do for ourselves what needs to be done for the sake of salvation. But from beginning to end in the gospel message is emphasized the fact that the human race is lost in sin and unable to save itself.

It is pointless to talk to anyone about the grace of God, the vicarious death of Jesus, and the gospel offer of salvation until that person's heart feels a keen sense of spiritual need. A soul is not ready to hear the sweet story of divine love until it has learned the bitter truth of human weakness and inability. Until this happens, a person is quick to sit in judgment on the rightness or wrongness of divine commands. He softens the requirement of repentance, dismisses baptism as unimportant, and tries to convince himself that a conscientious Christian life is required only of those who aspire to be leaders in the church. Such a person is not yet poor in spirit, for the poor in spirit delight in doing the will of the Father in heaven.

Take the case of Saul of Tarsus as an example. Saul is anything but poor in spirit when we first meet him in Scripture. He was proud of his Jewish heritage and sure that he was obtaining the Almighty's favor through the works of the Law of Moses. In his proud self-confidence, he blasphemed the name of Christ and persecuted any who wore that name. He had nothing but contempt for the gospel message and its demands.

Then something happened that was to transform his life totally. He saw the Lord on the Damascus Road and knew that all his self-righteous pride and works had been for nothing before God. He was put into a different frame of mind with reference to Christ than he had ever been in before.

In his new frame of mind, Saul was not proud and rebellious. To the contrary, he was now keenly aware of his spiritual poverty. Thus it was that when Ananias came to him three days later to tell him heaven's will for his salvation, he did not challenge or resist the instructions. "Rise and be baptized, and wash away your sins, calling on his name," said Ananias (Acts 22:16).

A few days before, Saul would have mocked the notion of baptism and its symbolic reference to Jesus' death. Now he was ready to submit to it. What accounts for the change? He had become poor in spirit. He had been made to realize that his only hope of salvation was in surrendering his will to the divine will.

How perfectly parallel Saul's experience is to that of many people today. I have discussed the Word of God with many people only to hear them ridicule the gospel and its requirements for their salvation. In particular, I have heard any number of people deny the necessity of baptism in God's will for human salvation. But I have never heard a man or woman who was poor in spirit make such a denial. In the case of a sincere person who is aware of his or her true condition before God, there is no sitting in judgment on the gospel. There is eager and willing obedience.

Second, one must be poor in spirit in order to live the Christian life successfully. Once a person has been humble enough to become a Christian through obedience to the gospel, what attitude should he or she take toward the new life as God's child? It must not be one of egotistical arrogance. It must not be that of a boastful Peter who told Jesus, "Even if I must die with you, I will not deny you" (Matthew 26:35). He did deny the Lord, not once but three times, on the very night of his arrogant statement.

Paul put into words the humble sense of confidence the Christian should have: "I can do all things in him who strengthens me" (Philippians 4:13). We need to have confidence in our ability to serve the Lord Jesus, but that confidence must be in him rather than ourselves. It must be Christ-confidence rather than self-confidence.

Third, entire churches must demonstrate humility in order to serve God acceptably.

The church at Laodicea was a proud church which said, "I am rich, I have prospered, and I need nothing." When Jesus gave that group an inspection, his verdict was different. He said, "You are wretched, pitiable, poor, blind, and naked" (Revelation 3:16). Some churches today remind us of Laodicea. They are proud of their beautiful buildings, indirect lighting, paved parking, carpets, padded pews, and the number of people on the roll – without being

17

aware of their spiritual impotence. They fail to realize that the real strength of the people of God is measured in faith rather than finances. This lesson may be needed more today than in the first century.

The Blessedness of the Poor in Spirit

What is the special happiness which comes to the poor in spirit? "Theirs is the kingdom of heaven," said Jesus.

Why do humble people receive the kingdom of heaven? The answer is extremely simple. *They are the only ones who seek the kingdom.* The proud person feels no urgency to find God; the humble one seeks him constantly. The former can never be blessed because his heart is closed to the grace of God; the latter will be blessed because he has emptied himself in order to have room for heavenly grace.

Conclusion

Most students of the Beatitudes consider poverty of spirit the root Beatitude from which all the others grow.

Surely it is true that without the spirit of deep humility which is envisioned in this statement, without a realization of our helplessness and utter dependence on God, we are in no state to receive the unsearchable riches of Christ.

"A man's pride will bring him low, but he who is lowly in spirit will obtain honor" (Proverbs 29:23).

Questions for Discussion

1. What spiritual blessings are (potentially) involved in material wealth? What spiritual problems?
2. What spiritual problems are (potentially) involved in material poverty? What spiritual blessings?
3. Does "Blessed are the poor in spirit" relate directly to either material wealth or poverty?
4. Discuss the comment of John Redhead on the meaning of "poor in spirit."

5. What are some of the more repulsive things associated with pride?
6. Discuss the Parable of the Pharisee and the Tax Collector in light of James 4:4-10.
7. Why is humility necessary in order for a sinner to be saved? ·
8. Show the necessity of this spirit for living the Christian life.
9. Is humility a virtue in the life of a congregation of believers? Explain your answer.
10. Why would some people regard this Beatitude as the foundation for all the others? What is your opinion?

3/ Happiness is Mourning

"Blessed are those who mourn, for they shall be comforted" (Matthew 5:4).

Christ and the world certainly have different standards of happiness. The world regards all mourning as unmitigated disaster and seeks to defend itself from any and all circumstances which would generate it. Thus it is that modern living places a premium on being able to isolate yourself from your neighbors or any responsibility to them. We don't want to be hurt, so we refuse to place confidence in others or to share in the sorrows that others experience.

When some inevitable heartache does come to an individual, the tendency is to try to evade it through drugs, alcohol, or a frenzy of meaningless activity.

We human beings just don't want to face up to the reality of pain, sorrow, and mourning – either in our own lives or in the lives of people around us.

In stark contrast with such an attitude, Jesus' standard for happiness demands that we accept painful reality and view it as a spiritual opportunity. Rather than develop defense mechanisms against mourning, the follower of

Christ faces it in faith and confidently expects to receive a blessing from it.

As in all things, Jesus is our perfect example. In order to walk in his steps, we must be willing to meet sorrow, grief, and mourning on life's path. The prophet Isaiah spoke of the Messiah's work among men and was guided by the Spirit of God to foresee that he would be "despised and rejected by men; a man of sorrows, and acquainted with grief" (Isaiah 53:3). Therefore it is imperative that we understand this Beatitude and learn to be the type mourner who can be blessed of God for his experience.

Mourning Without Profit

Don't get the wrong impression about the "blessedness of mourning." *Some mourning has no value at all.*

The New Testament makes a distinction between "godly sorrow" and "worldly sorrow." It is only those people who experience the former who have any spiritual benefit promised to them. Consider, for example, the words of Paul: "For godly grief produces a repentance that leads to salvation and brings no regret, but worldly grief produces death" (2 Corinthians 7:10).

What are some forms of grief, mourning, and sorrow which bring no profit?

First, some mourning is simply the result of having a gloomy attitude toward life. The world is full of people who cannot see good in anything or anybody. They live in continual depression and dejection. They are just *pessimists.*

I once heard a fable about two frogs, appropriately named Optimist and Pessimist, who fell into the same can of milk. With a sad face and voice choking with despair, Pessimist moaned that there was no hope for their survival, sank to the bottom, and died. Optimist kept on kicking, and when the can was opened the next morning he was sitting comfortably on the lump of butter his kicking had churned.

This silly little story illustrates the basic difference in disposition all of us see in the people we know. There is no virtue or joy in being a melancholy pessimist who complains constantly. This is a type of worldly sorrow which brings misery and death instead of happiness and life.

Second, the mourning of discontent over one's circumstances in this materialistic world is not the grief Jesus has promised to bless.

Advertising companies specialize in making people feel disenchanted. Our society is geared to constant competitiveness and the urge to "keep up with the Joneses." There are countless thousands who can be thrown into mourning over the fact that John Doe has a new automobile and his wife is wearing an expensive fur coat. Is this the type of sorrow to be encouraged? Is this the spirit the Lord will bless? Certainly not.

Jesus warned against becoming preoccupied with things of this life. He taught: "Take heed, and beware of all covetousness; for a man's life does not consist in the abundance of his possessions" (Luke 12:15). Paul wrote: "There is great gain in godliness with contentment; for we brought nothing into the world, and we cannot take anything out of the world; but if we have food and clothing, with these we shall be content" (1 Timothy 6:8). The ones among us whose lives are wrapped up in the things of this world and whose only real sorrows relate in some way to material loss and thwarted personal ambition are not the persons who will receive the Lord's blessings. To the contrary, they will likely be among the world's most unhappy people.

A third sort of mourning which is without spiritual value is that which results from having to bear the consequences of your own wicked deeds.

Many a thief mourns over the shame of being uncovered in his deed and having to spend time in jail. At the same time he is mourning over his situation, he may be planning a way to do the same thing in the future – without getting caught. The person involved is not sorry for committing an evil deed; he is only sorry that he got caught. Perhaps the sorrow a man feels is due to the fact that he is dying of cirrhosis of the liver and not that he has been an alcoholic for twenty years. Perhaps a woman feels deep sorrow over losing her family but has no regrets about her acts of adultery which brought about the loss. These hypothetical situations involve only "worldly grief" which brings death. Not one is an instance of the "godly grief" which brings about true repentance and spiritual happiness.

Mourners Who Are Blessed

Having looked at this Beatitude from the negative side, we still have the question of its real meaning to examine. Who are the mourners God will bless? The Bible points to four categories of sorrowing people who will receive the comfort and blessing of Almighty God.

First, God will comfort those who react to their personal sufferings and sorrows in steadfast faith.

"The problem of pain and suffering is as old as life itself, and the minds of men have attempted four solutions. The first is to deny the reality of suffering, to bury your head in the sand and refuse to see. That is the method of the Christian Scientist. I was talking with such a man once, and when I asked him what he did with the suffering of Jesus on the cross, he used a word I never heard before. He said, 'I just unsee it.' That calls for a mental trick of magic which I have never learned. The second solution is to count suffering an evil and seek to get rid of it by getting rid of the capacity to feel and therefore to suffer. That is the method of the Stoic, and it does violence to your humanity. The third solution is to regard suffering as the result of the will of God and submit to it, with the hope that in the end he will tip the scales in your favor. That is the method of the Mohammedan. The fourth solution is to accept trouble as a part of life and make something out of it. That is the method of the Christian." [John Redhead, *Finding Meaning in the Beatitudes*, pp. 26-27].

Pain and suffering are not inherently evil. They are simply a part of our world and can, when reacted to properly, serve a constructive purpose in what has been called the "soul-making process." They can serve, as they did with

Job, to purify a man's faith and cause him to trust God more completely than ever before.

Jesus taught his disciples to accept the inevitable fact of suffering in human experience when he said, "In the world you have tribulation." In the very same breath, however, he gave them encouragement designed to make them bold in the face of it. He continued, "But be of good cheer, I have overcome the world" (John 16:33). If we are going to follow in the steps of Jesus, we must walk with him through the dark valley of suffering.

What possible happiness or blessing can come of the experience of physical suffering?

For one thing, there is the happiness which comes of experiencing the comfort which God himself gives to the sufferer who has committed himself to his Faithful Creator. When one is in good health and relatively carefree, he may be prone to think of himself as a totally self-sufficient person. But in the full realization of his weakness which comes with suffering, that same person will abandon pride and be drawn closer to his Heavenly Father. In this state of humility and prayerfulness, he is able to experience the bounties of divine grace and be comforted.

For another, the sufferer is able to attain a proper set of life values. In good health and prosperity, a woman may think the world consists of nice clothing, respectable friends, and social graces. But in failing health or unaccustomed poverty, she is more likely to realize that spiritual considerations are the things of supreme importance.

Finally, suffering enables you to be more sympathetic toward others. A person who has never had to bear the full weight of sorrow's burden may dismiss another's cares lightly. One who has borne a similar sorrow can not only sympathize with the aching heart but can also give it meaningful encouragement.

Second, God blesses those who mourn over the afflictions of other people. The selfishness so typical of our species causes us to look only to ourselves and to disregard the needs of others. Jesus requires us to rise above this tendency and to love our neighbors as ourselves (Matthew 22:39). Paul urged Christians: "Let each of you look not only to his own interests, but also to the needs of others" (Philippians 2:4).

A seismograph is a delicate scientific instrument which measures and records vibrations in the earth's crust. In a similar way, the heart of a consecrated and caring child of God is a type of divine seismograph which registers and responds to the tremors of pain and sorrow which occur so constantly in its environment. Such a heart is one that can "weep with those that weep" (Romans 12:15). It does not cloister itself away from the world so as to be untouchable by its miseries and woes. Instead, in imitation of Christ, it is "moved with compassion" by the needs it sees and attempts to meet those needs with divine resources.

Christ, both by personal example and specific command, requires that those who wear his name shall not overlook the poor, blind, hungry, imprisoned, sick, and bereaved. Those who wear his name but manifest a heart that is calloused and insensitive to the sufferings of their world disgrace his name. Those who are tender and sensitive know the blessedness of becoming instruments of God for the bringing of his mercy and aid to the helpless and needy.

Third, God blesses those who mourn over their own sinfulness and spiritual unworthiness. Surely this is the primary meaning of the second Beatitude. The Son of God came among us and said, "I tell you, No; but unless you repent you will all likewise perish" (Luke 13:5). But no person will – or can – repent of sins for which he is not sorry. And his sorrow must be more than shallow regret or the pain which comes of having been exposed to friends and public view. It must be genuine remorse and agony of spirit over the realization that the will of God has been transgressed.

My personal fear is that the commonest concept of sin among people of our generation is a coldly intellectual one which will never bring about a situation of mourning. It is easy to admit imperfection and to admit having done wrong. But such admissions need not mean any more than the candid statement of a young man who frankly admitted certain sinful (and criminal) acts, only to add, "But so what?"

Receiving salvation begins with a keen sense of one's own sinfulness. Only the person who is intensely sorry for his or her sin, the one who is broken-hearted over it, will repent and flee to Christ for safety and pardon. James tied together the penitent plea and the forgiving response when he wrote: "Draw near to God and he will draw near to you. Cleanse your hands, you sinners, and purify your hearts, you men of double mind. Be wretched and mourn and weep. Let your laughter be turned to mourning and your joy to dejection. Humble yourselves before the Lord and he will exalt you" (James 4:8-10). This is the "godly grief" Paul wrote about which "produces a repentance that leads to salvation and brings no regret."

When a person is in a state of contrition and mourning for sin, he is a fit subject for conversion and salvation. He is no longer hiding under a cloak of self-righteousness and resisting the will of God. He realizes that submission to God is the only real hope for his salvation and joy. When – in deep sorrow over his sin – he hears the beautiful story of Jesus and his saving love, he responds eagerly in faith to receive it.

He renounces his old life of sin and commits himself to walking in the footsteps of Jesus from that time forward. Then, in order to have all his past sins removed forever, he confesses his faith in Christ and is baptized for the remission of sins. The people in Jerusalem who heard Peter preach on the first Pentecost following the resurrection of Jesus were convinced by his sermon that Jesus was the Son of God and convicted of their sinfulness in having been participants in his murder. The Bible says they were "cut to the heart." This is simply another way of saying that they were made to feel intensely sorry for what they had done. Then they asked Peter and the other apostles, "Brethren, what shall we do?" The answer given them was as follows: "Repent, and be baptized every one of you in the name of Jesus Christ for the forgiveness of your sins" (Acts 2:37-38). All who come to Christ by this simple gospel message have the comfort and happiness which comes of the knowledge they are saved, children of God, and heirs of eternal life.

Then, fourth, it should also be noted that God blesses those who mourn over the sins of others. The Savior himself once wept over the sinful city of Jerusalem (cf. Luke 19:41). Paul testified to the "great sorrow" and "unceasing anguish" he felt on behalf of his Jewish kinsmen who were yet unbelieving and therefore still lost in sin (Romans 9:1-5). The same apostle reprimanded the Christians at Corinth for their failure to mourn over the sins of one among their fellowship. "And you are arrogant! Ought you not rather to mourn? Let him who has done this be removed from among you," he said (1 Corinthians 5:2).

Christ and his earliest disciples were genuinely concerned about the physical needs of people around them. They acted in several instances to help satisfy those needs. But we must never let ourselves think that Christ's mission – or that of his church today – is primarily a humanitarian one. The foremost mission of Christ and his church is "to seek and to save the lost" (Luke 19:10).

The failure of many Christians and many congregations to be genuinely evangelistic is traceable to a lack of serious concern for and mourning over the sins of others. When we come to view others' sins as our own, we will begin to be more active in carrying the gospel message of love and pardon into the whole world.

Conclusion

Christians have the promise of divine aid and strength. We know that God will be with us in every circumstance of life.

If we think of the sins of the past, we are able to be happy in the knowledge that God has forgiven them through Christ. If we have pain and sorrow to bear now, we are happy in the knowledge that we are not alone with our grief. And if we think of death, we look to the blessed promise of a new and better life beyond. We have a great deal to be happy about!

The non-Christian is left to mourn all these things without any comfort or hope. He has nothing, for he does not have a Savior. Why would anyone reject Christ and forfeit the joy only he can give?

Questions for Discussion

1. How does this Beatitude remind you of the radically different standards for happiness which Christ and the world have?
2. What distinction does Paul make between "godly grief" and "worldly grief"?
3. Describe some situations of mourning which hold no promise of spiritual blessing.
4. Are pain and sorrow inherently evil? How have men tended to react to suffering? How should a Christian react? Cf. James 1:2-3, 12.
5. How does God bless the person who mourns over the afflictions and problems of other people?
6. How is this Beatitude related to the biblical doctrine of repentance?
7. Secure an acceptable definition of "repentance." Would it be correct to call this the most difficult human step in the redemption process?
8. What happiness comes to the penitent person?
9. What is it to mourn for the sins of other people?
10. How does the attitude of grief over the sins of other people show itself in a Christian's life?

4/ Happiness is Meekness

"Blessed are the meek, for they shall inherit the earth" (Matthew 5:5).

The Bible teaches that meekness is one of the fruits of the Spirit which every Christian ought to bear in his life (Galatians 5:23). It is one of the traits of character which Paul commended to the saints at Ephesus (Ephesians 4:2). Peter required that a Christian be prepared to make a defense of his faith "with meekness and fear" (1 Peter 3:15 ASV). Yet it would be interesting to know how many modern believers have ever prayed for the Lord to make us meek people.

Our common conception of meekness makes it a contemptible rather than admirable trait.

We generally associate meekness with weakness. Thus we use the expression "meek as a mouse" in a most unflattering way to refer to people who are morally weak and spineless. We probably tend to associate the term "meekness" with some character who lets everyone walk over him and take advantage of him in every situation. Very few of us would be inclined to use the term to describe the people we admire most.

The difficulty here lies in the fact that we want to be strong and courageous people, whereas meekness suggests weakness and surrender to most of us. The last thing the average person would like to be known for is his or her meekness.

Yet Jesus plainly taught that meekness is required of anyone who would be truly happy and "inherit the earth." How can it be? Is it possible that our conception of meekness is confused? Surely this Beatitude demands some very close study.

What Meekness is Not

The first thing which needs to be done in this study is to clear away some of the false notions which have become attached to the word "meekness."

Meekness is not another name for timidity. Some people are afraid of groups and institutions to the point they never question their beliefs or practices. They simply conform – even when something within them feels uneasy about such conformity. Timid youngsters will use bad language and participate in things they know are wrong rather than resist peer pressure. Men will be dishonest in their business dealings in order to keep a job with a company that operates on the shady side. People will continue to hold membership in denominations whose doctrines, organization, and worship are clearly different from those authorized in the New Testament rather than risk the disfavor of family or friends by questioning and challenging those unscriptural things.

Jesus of Nazareth was no timid man who simply went along with the crowd. He challenged the false religious teachers of his day and boldly denounced their hypocrisy. The first-century church was no collection of weaklings which conformed to the popular notion of religion. They turned the world upside down in one generation precisely because they were different from it. Paul charged: "Do not be conformed to this world but be transformed by the renewal of your mind, that you may prove what is the will of God, what is good and acceptable and perfect" (Romans

32

12:2). Souls who are so weak as to be unable either to have or to demonstrate conviction are not be be imitated but pitied.

Neither is meekness the pointless surrender of your rights (cf. Matthew 5:38-41). It is admirable to "turn the other cheek" to insults and taunts. It is a virtuous thing to forego a right willingly for the sake of providing some benefit to another or to avoid needless contentions (cf. 1 Corinthians 6:1-8). But these virtues must not be prostituted into vices by supposing there are no limits to what one must endure at the hands of ungodly and evil people. Consider some case studies of biblical incidents.

Paul was unjustly beaten and thrown into jail at Philippi. As a Roman citizen, he had suffered an indignity which his enemies and the city officials had no right to inflict. He insisted on his legal right of public exoneration when he said, "They have beaten us publicly, uncondemned, men who are Roman citizens, and have thrown us into prison; and do they now cast us out secretly? No! let them come themselves and take us out" (Acts 16:37).

Jesus himself insisted on his rights when an officer of the Temple guard struck him. "When he had said this, one of the officers standing by struck Jesus with his hand, saying, 'Is that how you answer the high priest?' Jesus answered him, 'If I have spoken wrongly, bear witness to the wrong; but if I have spoken rightly, why do you strike me?' " (John 18:22-23). Meekness does not require the forfeiture of one's legal and moral rights under law.

Furthermore it should be understood that meekness is not an easygoing indifference to truth and right. There are some people who would seek peace at any price. They are willing to compromise principle in order to avoid having to disagree with someone. Now the desire for peace is surely good within itself. But to sacrifice some clear truth of God in order to attain peace is simply too high a price to pay.

There is a great movement abroad in the religious world of our day for ecumenicity and union. Some have lauded the leaders of this movement as meek and pious men who are seeking to bring about the will of God. I cannot praise what has come to be known as the "ecumenical movement," for it is simply a form of spiritual compromise. It is an attempt to smother conviction and truth under an avalanche of platitudes about peace and harmony. And what some are calling meekness in this context is more nearly the absence of real conviction about the truth of God.

The meekness of which Jesus spoke is nothing resembling the weak and whining attitudes which have been discussed up to this point in our study. Only when we can get people to realize that meekness is not a form of contemptible weakness will we be able to get them to pursue this trait in their lives.

The truth of the matter is that *meekness is the exact opposite of weakness.* It is strength and power. It is mastery over our human nature.

The True Meaning of Meekness

The Greek word translated "meek" in the third Beatitude is a word which was used to refer to wild animals which had been tamed. This should begin to suggest something of the meaning which the word carries.

Suppose a man spots a beautiful wild stallion running free on a range. The animal is obviously powerful and full of energy, but it is useless so long as it is wild. It does not know what it is to carry a man or pull a load. But suppose further that the man who spots the horse pursues it and puts it in a corral. Ultimately the animal is calmed enough that it can be bridled and saddled. Now an expert rider mounts, and the horse begins to run and buck. After a while, it becomes apparent that the rider is in control. The horse has been "broken." It has been tamed, brought under control, made useful for some good purpose.

This illustrates something of what it is for a human being to learn to be meek. *Meekness is simply a will that has been tamed and brought under control.* Just as a wild horse is tamed and brought under its owner's control, so we human beings have to be tamed and brought under divine control. Thus it follows that a meek man is not a weak man; he is still a strong man but has now submitted himself to the controlling influence of God in his life. A meek woman is not a weak woman; she is one who has allowed her personality and will to be harnessed for the purposes of heaven in this world. Meekness is the taming of the wild animal within each of us and putting that power to work in God's kingdom.

You may be surprised to learn that Moses is described as the meekest man of his time. "Now the man Moses was very meek, more than all men that were on the face of the earth" (Numbers 12:3). Yet Moses was a man of such fiery passion that, while still a young man in Egypt, he killed an Egyptian when he saw him mistreating one of his Israelite brothers. At that point in his life, Moses did not have himself under control. But then he put his soul under the care and control of God, and his wild strength was tamed and put into spiritual harness for the work of God. Moses was no weakling. He was not a timid coward. He was a strong man under divine control. That is what it is to be meek.

Perhaps the best way to shed light on the meaning of meekness is to consider the fact that Jesus called himself "meek and lowly" (Matthew 11:29). Jesus was certainly no wave of the sea which was tossed to and fro by every wind that blew. He was a man of strong determination, strong words, and strong actions. He could be moved to intense anger by false men, false deeds, and false religion. Mark 10:14 tells how Jesus saw his disciples trying to prevent little children from being brought to him and was "indignant" over it. When the Pharisees and scribes sought to protest Jesus' healing the man with a withered hand on the sabbath, he "looked around at them with anger, grieved at their hardness of heart" (Mark 3:5).

Jesus of Nazareth had words of stern condemnation for those who would put stumblingblocks in the path of others (cf. Matthew 18:6ff). He denounced the Pharisees in no uncertain terms for their hypocrisy (Matthew 23). And his righteous indignation so moved him when he saw men profaning the Temple in Jerusalem that he overturned the chairs and tables of the merchants, turned animals loose, and drove men out of the Temple grounds (Mark 11:15-18). He was meek, yet he was possessed of energy and passion which surpass that of ordinary human beings.

What, then, is meekness? *Meekness is submission to divine control.* It is the conquering of a carnal mind and bringing it into a state of true spirituality. It is the subduing of fleshly lusts whereby your very body is made both pure and serviceable to God. It is the disposition of spirit which accepts God's will without disputing. It is a will that has been tamed and placed under the control of God.

Notice the progression taking place in the Beatitudes. The first one requires humility and a full realization of our need for salvation. As an individual becomes "poor in spirit," he sees Jesus as his only hope and comes to believe in him. The second requires mourning over our sins and inevitably leads to genuine repentance. The third commends submissiveness to the will of God.

Thus, in the first three Beatitudes, we have observed three essential steps toward our salvation – faith, repentance, and obedience.

Seen in this light, surely there is no one who can contend seriously that meekness is a form of weakness. *It is spiritual strength of the highest magnitude.* It is the willingness to be controlled by God in the midst of a world which is, at its best, indifferent to God and, at its worst, openly blasphemous and rebellious toward him.

Meekness Toward God

Paul traces the path of meekness toward God when he contrasts the state of one's life before conversion to that which follows. He writes: "Let not sin therefore reign in your mortal bodies, to make you obey their passions. Do not yield your members to sin as instruments of wickedness, but yield yourselves to God as men who have been brought from death to life, and your members to God as instruments of righteousness. For sin will have no dominion over you, since you are not under law but under grace"

(Romans 6:12-14). This is the story of salvation. A life once yielded to sin is now surrendered to God.

The practical test of meekness is accomplished by means of the Word of God and its demands upon us. Thus James wrote: "Therefore put away all filthiness and rank growth of wickedness and *receive with meekness the implanted word,* which is able to save your souls. But be doers of the word, and not hearers only, deceiving yourselves" (James 1:21-22). How does someone receive the word with meekness? The answer should be obvious from our previous study. One receives the word with meekness by allowing himself to be led and controlled by its divine directives. He receives the word with meekness by becoming a "doer of the word."

Can you honestly say your life demonstrates this spirit? Are you willingly submitting your will to divine control by means of obedience to the gospel of Christ? Or are you still resisting God?

Meekness is not only necessary for one's initial acceptance of the gospel whereby he becomes a Christian; it is also at the heart of a sound relationship with God as his child.

One who has become a child of God needs to view him as a Father who can be trusted without reservation. The Christian must commit everything to the care and guidance of his Heavenly Father in full confidence that it will be guarded against the last Great Day. In the face of trials, he remains faithful to God; confronted with temptation, he looks for divine strength to resist the evil one; in making decisions, he seeks to do God's will in everything. He has adopted this philosophy of life: "I have been crucified with Christ; it is no longer I who live, but Christ who lives in me; and the life I now live in the flesh I live by faith in the Son of God, who loved me and gave himself for me" (Galatians 2:20).

If this attitude of meekness toward God is present in your life, you will demonstrate a controlled spirit in all your dealings with people around you. "Remind them to be submissive to rulers and authorities, to be obedient, to be ready for any honest work, to speak evil of no one, to avoid quarreling, to be gentle, and to show perfect courtesy toward all men" (Titus 3:1-2). Be fair, courteous, and gentle with enemies as well as friends, with poor as well as rich, with those of another race as well as with those of your own.

In your meekness, you will have occasion to feel angry and indignant over certain things – as did Moses and Christ before you. But the control of your spirit by the Spirit of God will see to it that righteous indignation does not degenerate into evil hatred. Meekness no more demands easygoing indifference to sin in our world than it did in Christ's. The Word cautions: "Be angry but do not sin; do not let the sun go down on your anger, and give no opportunity to the devil" (Ephesians 4:26-27).

There must be anger in the Christian life, but it must be the right kind of anger. Drug trafficking, abortion, pornography, and fraud in government *should* make you angry because of what they mean in terms of rebellion against and disrespect for a Holy God.

Indignant over sin yet controlled by God, you can be a powerful force to help accomplish the heavenly purpose of bringing men to salvation and right living. If you ever lose the ability to be angry over the sin surrounding you, it will mean that you have lost your convictions and thus the ability to render effective service.

Conclusion

A life of Christian meekness demands the utmost moral courage and spiritual strength. *It is no life for moral cowards and spiritual weaklings.* To possess and demonstrate meekness is to enjoy both the abundant blessings of God and the healthy respect of people around you. Just as Christ's courageous meekness won him the admiration of even governor Pilate, so our meekness in loving our enemies, living our convictions, and serving our Lord will serve to make us the light of the world and the salt of the earth (Matthew 5:14-16).

The person who lives this type of life has heaven's joys to anticipate. Even in this life, he enjoys blessings no other person can receive from above. He both "inherits the earth" and receives a pledge of heaven in his meekness.

Questions for Discussion

1. Use a concordance to find several passages which speak of meekness. Notice the favorable use of the word throughout Scripture.
2. What is the general notion most people seem to have about this trait of character?
3. Was the Lord a weak and timid man? Was Paul? What does this imply about the common understanding of meekness?
4. Does meekness involve forfeiting one's legal and moral rights? Under what circumstances should a Christian "turn the other cheek"? When should he resist the evil person?
5. What is the history of the word translated "meek" in this Beatitude? What does this suggest as to the meaning of this trait?
6. Define "meekness" in such a way as to take account of the biblical perspective on this quality.
7. Does a correct definition of meekness suggest weakness? What do the examples of Moses and Jesus indicate about this?
8. Discuss Romans 6:12-13 in view of the things you have learned in this lesson.
9. Is it wrong for Christians to get angry? Why, or why not?
10. How can Christians demonstrate meekness in ordinary situations of life? At work? At home? In church relationships?

5/ Happiness is
Hunger and Thirst

"Blessed are those who hunger and thirst for righteousness, for they shall be satisfied" (Matthew 5:6).

No one ever achieved anything really worthwhile in life without the motivation of a burning desire. The desire to achieve makes a student successful in school. The desire to relieve suffering and restore health to people has inspired doctors and researchers to find cures and effective treatments for such dread diseases as smallpox, diptheria, polio, etc. The desire for rapid transportation brought about the modern jumbo jets which serve all parts of the world. All of these things were accomplished because an unsatisfied desire in the heart of someone cried out for fulfillment.

The fourth Beatitude is simply the application of this principle to spiritual living. "Those who hunger and thirst for righteousness" are, in simple terms, men and women who really want to live good lives which honor their Creator. Only those who really want to be righteous can ever attain that blessed state.

Most of us have occasional "cravings" for the better way of life presented in the Bible, but that is not enough motivation for actually attaining it. You will have to be motivated by a constant and deep desire (i.e., hunger and thirst) in order to be what God wants you to be.

The picture which Jesus paints in this Beatitude is really not a very pretty one to see. It shows someone ravenous with hunger, parched and panting with thirst, and tells us that when we long for righteousness as much as that person wants food and water, we can be among the Lord's blessed people. This imagery seems to mock our world of self-satisfied and complacent religion. It lets us know that we will never be righteous until we forsake the shallow life which most are content to lead and have within our hearts an urgent longing for Christ and the righteousness which is in him.

The psalmist expressed this sentiment of spiritual longing of which Jesus spoke in the fourth Beatitude in this way: "As a hart longs for flowing streams, so longs my soul for thee, O God. My soul thirsts for God, for the living God" (Psalm 42:1-2a). Isaiah wrote: "My soul yearns for thee in the night, my spirit within me earnestly seeks thee" (Isaiah 26:9a). And David used these words: "O God, thou art my God, I seek thee, my soul thirsts for thee; my flesh faints for thee, as in a dry and weary land where no water is" (Psalm 63:1).

Men and women are made in the image of God. We were made for his fellowship. And the truth of the matter is that no one of us can be genuinely happy so long as he seeks satisfaction for his spiritual longings among the sinful things of the world. Only when we acknowledge our spiritual longings and allow them to draw us unto God and his true righteousness can we experience the blessed life we seek.

What is Righteousness?

It is rather obvious that a person cannot desire something that he knows nothing about. You cannot want to be righteous until you learn that righteousness does exist and find out something of its nature. To this point in our study, we have used the word "righteousness" without defining it. We cannot go further without getting clear about the term.

Is righteousness simply a matter of living a good, clean life? Is it just the keeping of one's word, the paying of just debts, and the right treatment of one's family and neighbors? Now certainly all these things are related to righteousness, but the biblical use of the word goes far beyond this level of life.

The Greek word translated "righteousness" in this verse (*dikaiosune*) means "integrity, virtue, purity of life, uprightness, correctness of thinking, feeling and acting" [Thayer]. It has to do with "whatever has been appointed by God to be acknowledged and obeyed by man" [Vine]. The word is also used of that gracious gift of divine justification which is bestowed upon those who have surrendered themselves to Christ in faith.

Notice some New Testament instances of the use of this word. It is used to mean "integrity, virtue, purity of life" in such passages as Romans 6:13 and 2 Timothy 2:22. "Do not yield your members to sin as instruments of wickedness, but yield yourselves to God as men who have been brought from death to life, and your members to God as instruments of righteousness." "So shun youthful passions and aim at righteousness, faith, love, and peace, along with those who call upon the Lord from a pure heart."

The same word is used to refer to that which "has been appointed by God to be acknowledged and obeyed by man" in such passages as Matthew 3:15 and John 16:8. "But Jesus answered him, 'Let it be so now; for thus it is fitting for us to fulfil all righteousness.' "

"And when [the Holy Spirit] comes, he will convince the world of sin and righteousness and of judgment."

Finally, the word is used of the justification which God bestows as a free gift upon those whom he saves from sin in passages such as 2 Corinthians 5:21 and Romans 3:21-22. "For our sake he made him to be sin who knew no sin, so that in him we might become the righteousness of God." "But now the righteousness of God has been manifested apart from law, although the law and the prophets bear witness to it, the righteousness of God through faith in Jesus Christ for all who believe."

Now that we have seen how the word "righteousness" is used in the Word of God to refer to situations which are somewhat different from each other, we are left with the question of which type of righteousness the Lord had in mind as he gave this Beatitude.

For example, it would be altogether possible for a man to be virtuous and honest (thus "righteous" in the first sense of the word noted above) yet refuse to obey certain commands which are part of the revealed will of God (thus "unrighteous" in the second sense of the word above). Or it could be that a person keeps certain commands of the revealed will of God in his daily life (thus "righteous" in the second sense above) but has not yet surrendered himself to Christ for the justification he gives to such believers (thus "unrighteous" in the third sense above).

Which type of righteousness did the Lord Jesus have in mind? Does he want all men simply to be honest and morally upright? Does he want all men to receive the justification which God bestows as a free gift? Or does he want all of us to conform our lives to the pattern of righteous living which we commonly refer to as the Christian life? Just which part of this total system of righteousness does the Lord commend to us in the fourth Beatitude?

Perhaps the significance of the Lord's statement in this Beatitude can be presented most clearly by means of an illustration. Suppose a woman is physically hungry and thirsty. Let us further suppose that she goes into the house of a friend and sees a pitcher full of water and a fresh loaf of bread on the table beside it. She could ask for a glass of water and a couple of slices out of the loaf of bread. If she were totally famished, however, she might ask for everything on the table. The difference is in asking for a glass of water as opposed to the whole pitcher or for a slice of bread as opposed to the whole loaf.

The construction of the original Greek sentence in this verse makes Jesus' meaning on this point very clear and emphatic. He is commanding us to hunger and thirst for *the whole of righteousness* and not just a part. Our desire must be for *everything* that is involved in true righteousness. Our hunger must be for more than a slice or two off the loaf of righteousness, our thirst for more than just a sip from the pitcher.

As surely as the Lord Jesus is the bread of life (John 6:48-50, 58) and personally leads his followers unto fountains of waters of life (Revelation 7:17), our desire must be for nothing less than the full satisfaction of our every spiritual need through him.

The hope of eternal life depends on our willingness to abandon our self-willed and arrogant ways in order to throw ourselves on the mercy of God. We must submit ourselves to him by obeying the gospel in order to receive the righteousness he bestows on those whom he saves from sin by the blood of Jesus. Then, in living new lives as God's people on earth, we must flee the defilements of the world and be righteous by conforming our daily lives to Christ's holy pattern for living. This not only involves those most fundamental elements of righteousness such as moral purity, honesty, and integrity but the peculiar Christian virtues of love and compassion. This is the full righteousness for which we must nurture a passionate desire. This is what we must hunger and thirst for, if we would be filled from above.

Evidences of Righteousness

What are the evidences which point to this sort of true righteousness in our lives? What qualities demonstrate that our hunger and thirst have been satisfied?

First, there is the fact of your death to sin. Sin is what stands in direct opposition to righteousness. And if you are to be genuinely righteous before God and men, you must die to it. Paul presses this very point in the sixth chapter of Romans: "How can we who died to sin still live in it? Do you not know that all of us who have been baptized into Christ Jesus were baptized into his death? We were buried therefore with him by baptism into death, so that as Christ was raised from the dead by the glory of the Father, we too might walk in newness of life. For if we have been united with him in a death like his, we shall certainly be united with him in a resurrection like his. We know that our old self was crucified with him so that the sinful body might be destroyed, and we might no longer be enslaved to sin. For he who has died is free from sin" (Romans 6:2-7).

To die to sin is to turn away from the love and practice of it. It is to quit sin and to put oneself under the control of God. This is brought about in connection with the beautiful act of baptism. A person has quit trusting himself and has started trusting Christ, so that individual identifes with Christ in baptism in order to put off the body of sin (cf. Colossians 2:11-12).

Baptism is an expressive symbolic act which links a believer with the death, burial, and resurrection of Christ. But it is more than a mere symbol; it is an essential part of the salvation process by means of which one receives the remission of sins (Acts 2:38), puts on Christ (Galatians 3:26-27), and enters the kingdom of heaven (John 3:3-5) and body of Christ (1 Corinthians 12:13). Baptism has no intrinsic worth; its value is in the fact that, by decree of God, it is the time and place where the penitent believer is actually linked with the death of Christ in order to have the blood of the Son of God applied to his soul for cleansing. The cleansing is entirely by blood and not by the water of baptism itself (cf. 1 Peter 3:21). The justification which God bestows as a free gift is received in connection with this reenactment of Christ's death, burial, and resurrection.

Second, the imitation of Christ in the life of one who has become a child of God is righteousness. The New Testament teaches: "By this we may be sure that we are in him: he who says he abides in him ought to walk in the same way in which he walked" (1 John 2:5b-6).

Jesus was righteousness personified. If we would be partakers in righteousness, we must surely conform ourselves to him. And this process of conformity to Jesus begins with an attitude of heart. "Have this mind among yourselves, which you have in Christ Jesus," commanded Paul (Philippians 2:5). His heart was set on heavenly things and intent on doing the will of his Father in heaven. We must learn to live by that same disposition.

We must love one another, bear one another's burdens, serve each other's needs, carry the gospel to the lost, and show men and women around us the joys of living under the Lordship of Jesus. The exhibition of this attitude of dedication and these acts of obedience to the divine will are evidences of righteousness in your life.

The Failure of Desire

What a wonderful thing it would be if we humans would long for righteousness with as much urgent desire as we show for the trivial things of life. If men would only desire righteousness as much as a new car or a profit on an investment; if women would only desire righteousness as much as a new wardrobe or smaller waistline. What a difference there would be in the lives of us all.

Hardly any words could better express the strong desire we should have for righteousness than "hunger" and "thirst." Although few of us have experienced the pangs of starvation, those poor peasants of Palestine who heard Jesus as he first uttered this Beatitude could appreciate the imagery in full measure. It was rare for them to eat meat, and their hunger was rarely ever satisfied by the meager amount of food they could put on their tables. Much of their land was dry to the point of being parched, and streams and wells were few and far between. They knew the compelling nature of real hunger and thirst.

The person who would have the blessing of our Lord must crave righteousness in the same manner and to the same degree as a starving man craves food and water.

The story is told of a young man who went to a wise old man in his community to inquire of him about the right way to live. The wise man led him down to a river, and the two of them walked some distance into it. The young man, perhaps thinking that some sort of purification ritual or baptism was about to take place, did not resist the old man. After they reached a certain depth in the river, the wise man took hold of the young man, pushed him under the surface, and held his head submerged! Realizing that he would surely drown without air, the young man began to struggle with all his might to escape and get his head above the water. He finally managed to free himself from the old man's grip and thrust his head above the surface.

As he gulped in the precious air, the wise man said, "When you thought you were about to drown, what did you want more than anything else?"

"Air!" the young man responded.

The old man replied, "When you want righteousness as much as you wanted air just now, it will become a possibility for you. But not before."

This is simply another way of impressing the lesson our Savior taught in the fourth Beatitude.

Conclusion

Our world is on the verge of spiritual starvation. And the great pity of it all is that many who are starving do not even realize it.

It is possible for people to satisfy their sensation of physical hunger by eating substances which are totally lacking in food value – and die of malnutrition. This is something comparable to what is happening to the world in spiritual things. It is having its stomach filled with the husks of unspiritual religion which are neither nourishing nor fully satisfying to its spirit. It is being fed a weak and tasteless diet of moral platitudes and human philosophy when its real need is for the enriching and life-giving gospel of Christ. Only the person who realizes his need for Christ and his true righteousness can ever be filled.

"Jesus said to them, 'I am the bread of life; he who comes to me shall not hunger, and he who believes in me shall never thirst' " (John 6:35).

Questions for Discussion

1. What is the difference between an occasional craving for something and a burning desire?
2. What is the meaning of "hunger and thirst for righteousness"? Is this spirit generally characteristic of people? Of religious people?
3. What is the meaning of the word "righteousness"? Reflect on its different uses in certain texts.
4. What is the significance of "righteousness" in this Beatitude?
5. What is involved in "dying to sin"? How is this related to righteousness?
6. What is the significance of baptism to the religion of Jesus Christ?
7. How is one's imitation of Christ a part of true righteousness?
8. Discuss Philippians 2:5. What is involved in having "the mind of Christ"?
9. Why would this Beatitude have been particularly expressive to the people who first heard it?
10. What are the things for which our world has its strongest desire? How can we help redirect this desire toward righteousness?

6/ Happiness is Mercy

"Blessed are the merciful, for they shall obtain mercy" (Matthew 5:7).

In this fifth Beatitude, the Lord Jesus has censured severely one of the greatest sins of the human race – *selfishness*. The path to genuine happiness is blocked by this spirit. Self-centeredness must be overcome, if we would share in the spiritual blessedness which is the topic of the Beatitudes.

How many people have you known whose world began and ended within the narrow sphere of their own narrow interests? These people always speak more fluently when the topic of conversation gets around to the self-centered projects and plans with which their minds are filled. To be sure, all of us are somewhat prone to this attitude; we would probably be shocked to know just how many times in a day's ordinary conversations the personal possessive pronoun "my" is used. I want to tell about *me* and *my* house, *my* desire, *my* problem, *my* ambition, *my* anything.

The longer this spirit is tolerated and nurtured in our lives, the less sincere interest we are able to show to the needs and desires of others. But that is exactly what *mercy* is. It is getting out of the narrow confines of selfish interests and moving into the larger world of caring for others and attempting to understand and meet their needs.

Whenever the topic of selfishness comes up, the mind of a Bible student goes almost immediately to a certain rich man of whom the Lord spoke. This rich man is a classic example of selfishness and utter disregard for the needs of others. Read the parable again carefully and notice the frequency with which the personal pronouns "I," "me," and "my" appear.

"And he told them a parable, saying, 'The land of a rich man brought forth plentifully; and he thought to himself, "What shall I do, for I have nowhere to store my crops?" And he said, "I will do this: I will pull down my barns, and build larger ones; and there I will store all my grain and my goods. And I will say to my soul, Soul, you have ample goods laid up for many years; take your ease, eat, drink, be merry." But God said to him, "Fool! This night your soul is required of you; and the things you have prepared, whose will they be?" So is he who lays up treasure for himself, and is not rich toward God' " (Luke 12:16-21).

Is it difficult to envision such a selfish man as the one presented in this New Testament parable? Probably not, for there is a little of this spirit in each of us. Whether we master selfishness with mercy or become self-centered souls without the capacity for the merciful treatment of others depends on our own desires in the matter. But the Lord clearly says that only those who show mercy can receive divine mercy. Thus it becomes imperative that we learn about this trait and find ways to manifest it in our lives.

Some Preliminary Considerations

A popular definition of mercy is "compassion or forbearance shown toward an offender or subject." First offenders are frequently shown mercy by the court and put on probation. An officer of the court is then appointed to keep in touch with that person and to assist him in making his life useful in society. It is reported that a very high percentage of first offenders, especially juveniles, never appear in court the second time. Thus our legal system has shown that mercy extended to certain people pays a dividend both in the life of the individual concerned and in the corporate life of the community in which he lives.

The mercy of Christ toward sinners is certainly far greater than the mercy a judge can show a first offender in court. Divine mercy is not only granted to those who are just beginning to sin, the spiritual "first offender," but also to the hardened sinner whose entire life to date has been spent in service to Satan. Jesus requires his disciples to "love your enemies" (Matthew 5:44); he has shown the perfect example of this type of love by loving his enemies. He showers divine mercy upon any and all who turn away from their sin and submit themselves to his will.

The Bible is constantly calling attention to the mercy of God. Paul wrote: "But God, who is rich in mercy, out of the great love with which he loved us, even when we were dead through our trespasses, made us alive together with Christ (by grace you have been saved)" (Ephesians 2:4-5). "He saved us, not because of deeds done by us in righteousness, but in virtue of his own mercy, by the washing of regeneration and renewal in the Holy Spirit" (Titus 3:5).

The Bible also encourages us to seek the mercy which God offers so freely. "Let us then with confidence draw near to the throne of grace, that we may receive mercy and find grace to help in time of need" (Hebrews 4:16).

Then, going still further, the Bible commands those who have learned of and experienced the mercy of God to show similar mercy to those around us. Such is the teaching of the Beatitude we are studying now.

What Is Mercy?

The word translated "merciful" in this Beatitude means "to feel sympathy with the misery of another, and especially sympathy manifested in act" [Vine]. Notice that mercy is more than just sympathetic feelings. It is action. It is doing something positive to express your concern and sympathy.

The Bible certainly supports this definition of mercy. In the Parable of the Good Samaritan (Luke 10:25-37), the Samaritan is pictured as being "moved with compassion" toward the man who had been beaten and robbed on the Jericho Road. Of how much value would those feelings have been to the wounded man if he had not done something practical to help him? It was his work of binding up the man's wounds, carrying him to an inn, and arranging for his care that showed he was a merciful man. At the conclusion of Jesus' telling of this story, the man for whose benefit the story had been told observed correctly that the Samaritan "showed mercy" to the wounded man.

Luke's Gospel records the healing of ten lepers and begins the story this way: "And as he entered a village, he was met by ten lepers, who stood at a distance and lifted up their voices and said, 'Jesus, Master, have mercy on us' " (Luke 17:12-13). What did those men want when they asked for the *mercy* of the Son of God? His sympathy? A few kinds words? *They wanted action.* They wanted the healing of their diseased bodies by his miraculous power.

When the publican prayed so penitently, "God, be merciful to me a sinner!" (Luke 18:13), he was asking for more than God's tender feelings of pity. He was asking for something to be done about his sins. He was asking for forgiveness.

What is the point of all these episodes from the New Testament? They all point to the fact that mercy is compassion and sympathy put into concrete actions. Mercy is not mere idle sentiment or vain words. It is taking positive action which will help someone in trouble. This puts a totally new perspective on the quality of mercy for some of us. It means that we must do more than merely feel sorry for people who are destitute and starving; we must do something to feed them. It means that we must do more than pray for the Lord to send missionaries to save the lost; more of us must become missionaries in our own home communities or even allow God to take us to some distant corner of the world to carry the saving good news of Jesus to those lost souls.

Furthermore, it should be observed that Jesus showed mercy to men in *personal* ways. He did not merely send a check to the Jerusalem Leprosy Fund and assume his responsibility to lepers had been met. He did not speak a few encouraging words to his disciples and send them out alone to preach to tax collectors and prostitutes. He personally attended to the same things he commanded others to do.

Jesus set an example for us by his own merciful deeds. He went to the homes of sinners, ate at their tables, and talked with them directly about repentance unto life. He did not merely love suffering and lost humanity *in general*; he showed his love and mercy to *specific individuals* in concrete deeds.

Today's Christian who gives a few dollars to help pay someone's hospital bill and a few more to a missionary who is going to Europe may be content to stop there. He may use these token gestures as salve for his conscience in order to excuse himself from having to go next door to help a neighbor. That is a poor brand of religion!

A Perfect Example

As with each of the Beatitudes, this virtue is seen in its purest form in the life of Christ. The specific case of the healing of the ten lepers referred to earlier is surely an example of his mercy. But think for a moment in much broader terms of the whole life and ministry of the Son of God. His very act of coming into the world to die for our sins and to open the path to the Father was his greatest exhibition of mercy.

Before you can sympathize with another person to the degree of being a real help and comfort to him, you must begin to "get inside his shoes." Before you can be genuinely sympathetic toward a hungry person, for example, you must have felt intense hunger at some time in your own experience. Before you can be sympathetic toward someone standing in the icy cold of a winter's day, you must have felt the agony of intense pain yourself at some time. Similarly, before you can be truly sympathetic toward a lost sinner, you must have experienced intense pain and agony over your own sins prior to your salvation.

When Jesus came as the Son of Man, he was "getting inside our shoes." He was putting himself in position to sympathize with our mortality and weakness in the fullest manner possible. "For we have not a high priest who is unable to sympathize with our weaknesses, but one who in every respect has been tempted as we are, yet without sinning" (Hebrews 4:15). Since Jesus has been where we are, he can sympathize with our predicament.

Jesus demonstrated divine mercy toward us when he took our sins upon himself and died to reconcile us unto deity. In giving the gospel through the inspired messages of apostles and prophets, he was making that mercy complete by offering us salvation through our living faith in him. Yes, he stood in our shoes, sympathized with our condition, and *took action to help us*. That was mercy in its most perfect exhibition.

A Parable

The Lord spoke a parable which has to do with this subject of mercy. In Matthew 18:21-35, he told of a certain man who owed his king ten thousand talents of silver. The man was unable to pay his enormous debt and pleaded for the king's patience. Moved with compassion for the poor man, the king forgave him the entire amount of his debt. Then, only a short while later, that same man came upon someone who owed him a rather insignificant amount. He became indignant and demanded full payment immediately. Refusing the poor man's pleas for patience and mercy, he threw him into debtor's prison until the account was settled. When the king heard what this ungrateful wretch had done, he called him back to his chambers and said, "You wicked servant! I forgave you all that debt because you besought me; and should not you have had mercy on your fellow servant, as I had mercy on you?"

The great debtor in this parable represents humankind, and the merciful king represents God. Man, by virtue of his sin against God, is a debtor to him (Isaiah 59:1-2). The debt is so great that payment is impossible. Thus Christ paid the debt for our sins and allowed us to be forgiven and saved by divine grace. When we receive Christ and are saved, God cancels the entire debt we owe. But the point of major emphasis in this parable is actually on the next issue it raises. What should be the attitude of a forgiven sinner toward those who may offend or sin against him? The Lord was teaching very emphatically that *one who has received mercy must show mercy.*

One of the concrete ways in which a Christian shows mercy is in his willingness to forgive others. This is the point Jesus stressed with Peter when he spoke the parable just cited. Peter was of the opinion that to forgive someone seven times was liberal enough. The Lord indicated that our forgiveness of one another should be unlimited. He also taught: "For if you forgive men their trespasses, your heavenly Father also will forgive you; but if you do not forgive men their trespasses, neither will your Father forgive your trespasses" (Matthew 6:14-15).

Another way to show mercy to others is to pray for them. "First of all, then, I urge that supplications, prayers, intercessions, and thanksgivings be made for all men, for kings and all who are in high positions ..." (1 Timothy 2:1-2). If we have compassion and true sympathy for others in their need, we will make earnest intercession for them with the Father in heaven.

Then surely there is no greater demonstration of mercy than for us to strive to lead men unto the salvation which is in Christ. James wrote: "My brethren, if any one among you wanders from the truth and some one brings him back, let him know that whoever brings back a sinner from the error of his way will save his soul from death and will cover a multitude of sins" (James 5:19-20).

Imitating our Lord, we must be concerned for the physical welfare of those who are sick, hungry, thirsty, unclothed, or in prison. But we must never allow our mercy to become so narrow in scope that it focuses only on physical needs. Jesus met the physical needs of people with a primary view toward their souls. This must be our procedure, too. In actions of kindness and mercy, Christians today should care for the physical needs of people around us and thereby gain a favorable hearing for the gospel, God's power to save both us and them. Thus attention has been paid to the whole man –body and spirit.

Conclusion

Does mercy bring a reward? Indeed it does! "Blessed are the merciful, *for they shall obtain mercy,*" said Jesus. Those who show mercy toward their fellows are in position to receive even greater mercies from on high.

In the day of final Judgment, God will not forget to repay the compassionate Christian who has shown mercy to others. But the poor soul who has shown no mercy toward others will receive no mercy from God in that day. "For judgment is without mercy to one who has shown no mercy; yet mercy triumphs over judgment" (James 2:13).

Christ wants men and women to be compassionate and merciful toward one another. Before we can do this, however, we must first receive the mercy extended to us through the gospel.

God longs to be merciful to each of us and to allow his mercy to reach to others through our lives. Will you allow it to happen in your life?

Questions for Discussion

1. What sin is condemned by this Beatitude? Is this sin characteristic at all of our generation?
2. Discuss the parable of Luke 12:16-19. How many of the Lord's parables touch on the same thesis?
3. What has our legal system demonstrated about mercy shown to first offenders? Trace some of the implications of this fact for Christianity.

4. Use your concordance to find additional passages about the mercy of God to sinners.
5. Define the word "merciful" used in this Beatitude. Give your own illustration of it.
6. Comment on the *personal* character of mercy. Are we too prone to practice this virtue by proxy?
7. What is the principal point of emphasis in the parable related in Matthew 18:21-35?
8. Name some specific ways a Christian can go about the business of showing mercy to others.
9. What reward comes to the person who learns to show mercy to others?
10. Can one who has not experienced the mercy of God in his own life show full and true mercy to others?

7/ Happiness is a Pure Heart

"Blessed are the pure in heart, for they shall see God" (Matthew 5:8).

The goal of humanity's religious aspirations and strivings is to see God (cf. Isaiah 33:17; 1 John 3:2). Yet the Lord makes it clear that only those who are "pure in heart" will realize that goal.

Many individuals are separated from God in this life by their sin (Isaiah 59:1-2), and all those who persist in their sin will be separated from him throughout eternity (2 Thessalonians 1:7-9). It follows that, since all those who will see God are pure in heart, no one will see him whose heart is not purified by divine power. Thus it becomes imperative that we learn what this purity is and how to attain it.

The "Heart" of Man

When we use the word "heart," we generally think of the muscular organ in our physical bodies which serves as a powerful pump to circulate the blood. People of both ancient and modern times have almost universally regarded it as the most important organ of the body, for when the heart ceases to function the entire body dies. Although the word is used a number of times in the Bible to refer to this physical organ, it is most often used in a manner which rules out the possibility of such a meaning. For example, the Bible speaks of a heart which can be "bitter" (Proverbs 14:10), "broken and contrite" (Psalm 51:17), "melted" (Psalm 22:14), etc. These adjectives would be without meaning if applied to a fleshly organ.

Surely it is unnecessary to offer detailed proof of the fact that Jesus was not predicating salvation upon the condition of one's fleshly heart. Who could believe that our Lord made freedom from heart disease a condition of eternal life? The very notion is absurd.

As the word "heart" is most often used in Scripture, it refers to a spiritual rather than physical aspect of our being. The word refers to the real personality of an individual, his "inner man" (cf. 1 Peter 3:4). As it is used in this Beatitude, it signifies a human being's total intellectual, emotional, and moral nature.

What, then, was the Lord saying in this Beatitude? He told us that happiness depends on the purity not of the outward or fleshly person but of our total character and personality. He was putting us on notice that acceptable religion involves more than carefully performed ritual, that it involves the very depths of our being.

The heart is the key to the whole person. The thoughts, desires, and purposes of the inner man determine the words and actions of the outer man. The author of Proverbs 4:23 wrote by inspiration and said: "Keep your heart with all vigilance; for from it flow the springs of life." The Lord Jesus added his own word of confirmation to this statement of truth when he observed: "For out of the heart come evil thoughts, murder, adultery, fornication, theft, false witness, slander" (Matthew 15:19). Any trait which ultimately becomes apparent in a person's behavior, whether good or bad, was first in his heart. The tragedy is not that it "slipped out" but that it was in his heart to begin with.

Since every action of our lives stems from the guidance of our hearts, it is apparent that we need divine guidance in purifying our hearts and committing them to the correct course of righteous living before God. We cannot trust the natural or instinctive desires of our hearts, for "the heart is deceitful above all things, and desperately corrupt" (Jeremiah 17:9). But our God has the power to "search the mind" and "try the heart" of humans in order to direct our lives in harmony with his will (Jeremiah 17:10; cf. 10:23).

What Real Purity Is

In trying to understand the *purity* of heart Jesus wants in his followers, we must not make the mistake of the Pharisees and scribes of his day who considered it to consist of ceremonial cleansings and exacting rituals. Hear again the words of stern rebuke addressed to those people by our Lord: "Woe to you, scribes and Pharisees, hypocrites! for you cleanse the outside of the cup and of the plate, but inside they are full of extortion and rapacity. You blind Pharisee! first cleanse the inside of the cup and of the plate, that the outside also may be clean. Woe to you, scribes and Pharisees, hypocrites! for you are like whitewashed tombs, which outwardly appear beautiful, but within they are full of dead men's bones and all uncleanness. So you also outwardly appear righteous to men, but within you are full of hypocrisy and iniquity" (Matthew 23:25-28).

Jesus used forceful satire to bring home his point about the purity demanded by true religion. Imagine a person who washes only the outside of a cup or bowl and leaves the inside dirty. What wisdom does that person demonstrate? What honor is he or she due? By the same token, what of religious people who are so particular to offer the correct sacrifice to the Lord on the right day and in the right place yet who come to the altar with the blood of innocent people on their hands? Can there be any value in such worship? It is of no more value to the taking away of sins than the whitewashing of a tomb is to the cleansing of the decay within it.

Our Savior was severe with the sin of hypocrisy during

his time among men. He demanded purity of heart as well as correctness of form in the worship of the Father.

Lest we act too hastily to point the finger of accusation at the scribes and Pharisees of Jesus' time, let us look into our own concept of religious purity. Do some of us not consider attendance at church gatherings the ultimate test of purity? Within the shadows of our buildings, however, people are going to bed hungry at night and know nothing of the Word of God that can save their souls.

Even the benevolent and evangelistic work we do undertake will be worthless without a correct motivation for doing them. Paul said that even such great works as speaking in tongues, prophesying, bestowing gifts upon the poor, and laying down one's life as a martyr are without profit before God unless motivated by love (1 Corinthians 13:1-3). Our hearts must be pure in all we do in the name of the Lord Jesus Christ!

First, true purity involves moral cleanness. John tells us that heaven is a place where no impurities can enter. "But nothing unclean shall enter it, nor any one who practices abomination or falsehood, but only those who are written in the Lamb's book of life" (Revelation 21:27). If we would enter this holiest of places, our hearts must be cleansed of their wickedness and deceitfulness.

How do we receive this spiritual cleansing? It does not come by our good works or meritorious efforts. We cannot purify our own hearts. The power to remove sin and its defilement belongs to Christ alone. "You know that he appeared to take away sins, and in him there is no sin" (1 John 3:5). It is the power of his blood which serves to wash away our sins. In the Revelation, John saw a great host of the redeemed who had "washed their robes and made them white in the blood of the Lamb" (Revelation 7:14). But does his blood cleanse everyone? Certainly not! What is the distinction, then, between purified and unpurified hearts?

Peter discussed the cleansing of human hearts and wrote: "Having purified your souls by your obedience to the truth for a sincere love of the brethren, love one another earnestly from the heart" (1 Peter 1:22). This statement clearly shows that there is a responsibility borne by each individual for the cleansing of his or her own heart. Only Christ's blood can provide purification, but we show our willingness to have his pardon by means of our obedience to the truth.

Prior to one's conversion, sin rules the heart. Evil thoughts and shameful desires dwell there. Disobedience and impenitence reign in an unregenerated heart (Romans 2:5).

Conversion is the process in which a heart is opened, turned around, and reoriented in all its priorities. The knowledge of Christ is like a light shining in one's heart (cf. 2 Corinthians 4:6). It has power not only to enlighten but to open a heart. When one receives Christ and identifies with him in baptism, the Spirit of God is sent into that individual's heart (Galatians 4:6). God pours his love into that heart and initiates the process of transformation that will continue for a lifetime.

The focus of a spiritual life is on spiritual things. The saved person points his heart, soul, and mind heavenward. With his citizenship now in heaven, everything centers there. "If then you have been raised with Christ, seek the things that are above, where Christ is, seated at the right hand of God. Set your minds on things that are above, not on things that are on earth" (Colossians 3:1-2).

The power to save and transform human beings is divine. But the choice as to one's heart orientation is a human choice. Salvation and transformation will not occur within a personality which is turned to all the wrong sources.

Once your heart has been cleansed by the blood of Christ, a new and different life can begin. "For out of the abundance of the heart the mouth speaks. The good man out of his good treasure brings forth good," said Jesus (Matthew 12:34-35). With a heart cleansed of all its sin, you can begin to bring forth good words, good motives, and good deeds from the inner you.

Second, true purity of heart involves the total consecration of your heart to God and his will. It requires convictions that are sincere and unmixed with any sort of unworthy motivation.

The word translated "pure" in this Beatitude (*katharos*) not only signifies that which is "pure, as being cleansed" but also that which is without the "admixture of any element" [Vine]. The word was used by people of Jesus' own time to signify substances such as gold or milk which were without any sort of foreign substance. For example, it was not unusual for a vendor to take a gallon of milk and mix it with chalky water in order to increase the amount of his product and thus his profit. Such milk mixed with a foreign substance was not pure. Gold was sometimes alloyed by the addition of another metal. Once the jeweler had done this with his gold, he was not selling pure gold any longer.

In the same manner, God intends that men serve him with unmixed motives. He wants hearts that are devoted to the single aim of his glory. Paul spoke of a single aim which motivated his life in 2 Corinthians 5:9. "So whether we are at home or away, we make it our aim to please him." In the same connection, he wrote: "So, whether you eat or drink, or whatever you do, do all to the glory of God" (1 Corinthians 10:31). Such single-minded sentiments must be our own, if we are to be "pure in heart."

One author put it this way: "By 'pure in heart' who can doubt that our Lord meant single-minded – the man who has one clear purpose, who is not, like so many of us, of mixed purposes? Most of us in the abstract want to do what is right, but we want to do it in such a way that it will dovetail nicely in with the mosaic of our lives, with our worldly and selfish or purely utilitarian aims. We want to mix a little or a good deal of this world with our other-worldliness. Only the man who is truly 'pure in heart' is free from this taint of mixed motives. His one desire is the seeing of the Good and following it."

This sort of purity of heart demands intellectual honesty. This means that we must receive the truth without any addition of false philosophy or human speculation. We must be content to learn the will of the Father as it is revealed in the Bible and submit ourselves to it. Such purity also demands the concentration of attention and affection on spiritual things. Think back to a passage already cited in this chapter: "If then you have been raised with Christ, seek the things that are above, where Christ is, seated at the right hand of God. Set your minds on things that are above, not on things that are on earth" (Colossians 3:1-2). This sort of committment to purity also demands a special excellence in character. Not only must we keep ourselves from evil deeds, but we must also come to desire righteousness with our whole hearts. We must come to view our religion as a delight and find our greatest happiness in the performance of our duties to God.

The heart which has attained this intellectual, emotional, and moral devotion to spiritual things is a "pure heart" in the sense spoken of by our Lord in the sixth Beatitude.

Conclusion

Finally, think about the results of this sort of purity. Just what comes from having a heart which is both morally pure and consecrated to God?

First, there is the obvious result that such a man's life will be pure before the Father. Just as an evil heart produces an evil life, so a pure heart produces a righteous life. The pure heart does not allow itself to be driven by hatred, jealousy, and greed. It does not envy another's success or good fortune. This kind of heart can offer pure worship to God, because it is totally consecrated to him.

Second, by the Lord's own promise, the pure in heart "shall see God." Does this mean that the pure in heart will be allowed to see the Lord face to face in heaven when this life is finished? Certainly it does, for John wrote: "Beloved, we are God's children now; it does not yet appear what we shall be, but we know that when he appears we shall be like him, for we shall see him as he is" (1 John 3:2). But it means more than this. It also means that we will "see God" in this life. We will not see him with physical eyes, but we will be able to see him in the world he has created, in the events of history, and in the workings of his divine providence in our own lives.

Is your heart pure because of cleansing by the blood of Christ? Have you consecrated your every spiritual thought and energy to the doing of the will of your Father in heaven? Why wait another day to receive his cleansing? Why postpone for one more day your commitment to the doing of his will in all things?

Questions for Discussion

1. What reward is promised to the pure in heart?
2. What is the meaning of "see God"? (Note: Compare the use of "see" by Jesus in John 3:3-5.)
3. What is the "heart" referred to by this Beatitude?
4. Why is purity of heart so important?
5. What did the Jews of Jesus' time think of as "purity"? How did Jesus address himself to this view?
6. Does any of the ancient Pharisaic concept of purity survive among us?
7. What are the two elements of biblical purity? Discuss each.
8. What is a human being's responsibility with regard to cleansing from sin? Can anyone other than Christ forgive sin? Can he forgive sin against our will?
9. Who is a "single-minded" Christian? How does this Beatitude relate to such a person?
10. Is one "pure in heart" if he lacks either of the two elements of purity identified in this lesson?

8/ Happiness is Making Peace

"Blessed are the peacemakers, for they shall be called sons of God" (Matthew 5:9).

Humanity has ever longed for the experience of genuine and lasting peace. But, because of the wickedness of the race, the goal has always escaped us. The Bible makes it plain that part of God's punishment upon the wicked is his denial of peace to them. "There is no peace, says the Lord, for the wicked" (Isaiah 48:22). On the other hand, Scripture emphasizes that part of God's blessing upon the righteous is the gift of peace. "Jehovah will give strength unto his people; Jehovah will bless his people with peace" (Psalm 29:11 ASV).

In Jesus' own day the world was tragically divided by conflict. For, even though the Roman armies had brought an end to armed conflict throughout the world, the hatred between men of different races, nationalities, and religions was in evidence everywhere. Jews and Gentiles regarded each other with mutual disgust and disdain. Citizens of the empire looked upon foreigners as pitiable creatures of inferior worth. The monied people of his time literally bought and sold human flesh without regard for individual rights or divine morality.

Today we see the same meanness and cruelty that existed in antiquity working to keep the fires of human conflict burning. Nations war with one another and apparently have no hesitation about breaking treaties of peace or promises of goodwill to each other. Within our own country there are groups of dissidents who are intent on agitating strife among our citizens. And many homes are centers of hatred and abuse rather than havens of love and peace.

Surely our world needs more men and women who are eager and earnest about the making of peace where there is strife. It is upon such people (i.e., the peacemakers) that the Lord's blessings will descend.

What is Peace?

Our study of this Beatitude must begin with a definition of the word "peace." As is so often the case, the Lord's idea about a given subject does not agree with the world's notion. Concerning the peace he gives, Jesus said, "Peace I leave with you; my peace I give to you; not as the world gives do I give to you. Let not your hearts be troubled, neither let them be afraid" (John 14:27). The peace which comes to men through Jesus Christ is not the same thing that people of the world seek in the name of peace.

The world generally thinks of peace in terms of personal contentment. Most people believe they would know real peace if only they could have no financial burdens, own a confortable home in a quiet neighborhood, and enjoy the restful company of family and friends at their convenience. If peace is nothing more than this, it is a retreat from reality which satisfies our selfish desires.

It may be that others think of peace in terms of compromise with the enemy. Surely it is possible to have a sort of peace by simply giving up the struggle and supposing that anything is better than the demanding task of having to fight for something. One author used to say that the only way to get rid of temptation was to yield to it. There is no peace in this sort of spineless submission to evil. "Peace at any price" usually turns out to be a cruel form of slavery.

The peace of which the Savior spoke so often is much more than the mere cessation of open hostilities with the enemy. It is more than the attitude of "live and let live." A husband and wife may not be fighting with fists or cruel words. They may be simply tolerating each other in stony silence and indifference. That is not peace either.

Our Lord gives peace, but "not as the world gives."

The Greek word for peace is *eirene*; the Hebrew word is *shalom*.

Shalom is the traditional Hebrew greeting or farewell. This word was never used to signify the mere absence of fighting. It is a term used for a positive state as opposed to a negative one. It means completeness or wholeness; it embraces everything which makes for a person's highest good.

But it is apparent that Jesus has a particular type of peace in mind in this Beatitude. He is talking about peace in the sense of right relationships among human beings. Further, the blessing promised in the Beatitude is not for those who merely *love* or *prefer* peace but for those who *make* peace.

Some people are quarrelsome and contentious troublemakers. They stir up strife in families, communities, and churches where their influence is felt. Such people are doing the work of Satan on earth. But those godly men and women who work to eliminate bitterness among their fellows and unite people in love and goodwill are doing the work of God. The troublemakers will always reap the fruits of their labors in strife and unhappiness. The peacemakers will experience the happiness which comes of sharing in the efforts of God to bring about harmony.

Three Dimensions of Peace

This Beatitude promises happiness to the person who works to make peace between estranged parties. But peace has three dimensions.

There is peace between man and God; there is inner peace which comes to the heart of God's child; and there is peace between a man and his neighbors. While this Beatitude focuses on the last of these, it clearly presupposes the other two. An individual has very little hope of success in attempting to make peace among the people of his world until he has first experienced peace with God and his own heart. Let us look briefly at each of these dimensions of peace.

First, there is the matter of an individual's right relationship with God. Salvation is the process of reconciling men to God. Paul wrote: "And you, who once were estranged and hostile in mind, doing evil deeds, he has now reconciled in his body of flesh by his death, in order to present you holy and blameless and irreproachable before him" (Colossians 1:21-22). Again, "All this is from God, who through Christ reconciled us to himself and gave us the ministry of reconciliation; that is, God was in Christ reconciling the world to himself, not counting their trespasses against them, and entrusting to us the message of reconciliation" (2 Corinthians 5:18-19).

When someone is still in sin, that person is counted as God's enemy (cf. Romans 5:10). It is sin that separates man from God and denies him peace. It was the mission of Christ to bring about reconciliation and peace "by the blood of his cross" (Colossians 1:20). Thus Christ is himself the world's greatest peacemaker, for he has made it possible for humans to be admitted again to the favor of our Heavenly Father. "Therefore, since we are justified by faith, we have peace with God through our Lord Jesus Christ" (Romans 5:1). Obedient faith in Christ brings one to a state of reconciliation and peace with God.

Second, there is the matter of inner peace with one's own self. Within the heart of every one of us are conflicting forces of good and evil. These forces pull us in opposite directions at the same time and turn us into "walking civil wars." We cannot have peace within our hearts while trying to serve two masters. Only the truly converted person who has "crucified the flesh with its passions and desires"

(Galatians 5:24) and who has surrendered himself to Christ's will for his life can experience real peace of mind. He can cease his inner fighting against God and say, "It is no longer I who live, but Christ who lives in me" (Galatians 2:20).

We must be totally honest with our hearts before God, if we would know the sort of inner peace under consideration here. We need to examine our lives in the light of God's Word to see whether or not we have done what God requires for our salvation. We need to be honest about the way we live before him as Christians. From the New Testament, we learn that man makes his peace with God and his inner man through childlike faith in God. Or, to say it another way, peace with God is possible only through one's unconditional surrender to God on divine terms.

It is only when these two dimensions of peace have been realized by an individual that he is ready to experience the third. That is, only after he has peace with God and himself can he make real peace with people around him. A person torn within his own soul about his salvation and personal peace of mind cannot be a peacemaker. But the one who has been reconciled to God and caused to be at peace within his own heart through Christ can also receive the peace heaven creates between human hearts. "But now in Christ Jesus you who once were far off have been brought near in the blood of Christ. For he is our peace, who has made us both one, and has broken down the dividing wall of hostility, by abolishing in his flesh the law of commandments and ordinances, that he might create in himself one new man in place of the two, so making peace, and might reconcile us both to God in one body through the cross, thereby bringing the hostility to an end" (Ephesians 2:13-16).

Jesus Christ brings saved people together in peace with one another. He breaks down the barriers between Jew and Greek, black and white, rich and poor, and he reconciles them all "in one body." That one body of Christ is his church (Colossians 1:18). Thus it is the Lord's intention for people to be at peace with one another and to live as brothers and sisters to each other in his church. So it has to be one of the saddest spectacles in the world to see people who claim to be Christians – thus brothers and sisters in the Lord – fighting with one another. They may, and certainly must, fight sin and error. But they must not fight one another. Christians are under obligation to "maintain the unity of the spirit in the bond of peace" (Ephesians 4:3).

Christians not only seek peace among themselves but with all people. "Strive for peace with all men" is the counsel of Hebrews 12:14. We are being peacemakers when we love people enough to proclaim the glorious message of salvation through Jesus Christ, the Prince of Peace, to them. We are being peacemakers when we show an eager willingness to forgive those who sin against us. We are being peacemakers when we live in humility and love with all people.

The Reward of the Peacemaker

The reward promised to the individual who heeds the seventh Beatitude and thus becomes a peacemaker is a magnificent one. "Blessed are the peacemakers, *for they shall be called sons of God.*"

The New Testament frequently refers to God as the God of peace (cf. Romans 15:13; 16:20; Hebrews 13:20). Since peace is so much a part of the character and work of God, no person could be his child who did not share this attribute.

The world may misunderstand the efforts of a peacemaker. People may try to take advantage of him. He may have to suffer ridicule from people who are bent on achieving evil purposes which run directly counter to the business of peacemaking. In the eyes of his Heavenly Father, however, he will be viewed as a son. And in the Last Day, he will be acknowledged publicly and rewarded as a son.

Another brief passage from the Sermon on the Mount will serve as a good commentary on this point. "You have heard that it was said, 'You shall love your neighbor and hate your enemy.' But I say to you, Love your enemies and pray for those who persecute you, *so that you may be sons of your Father who is in heaven*; for he makes his sun rise on the evil and on the good, and sends rain on the just and on the unjust" (Matthew 5:43-45). Christians who love their enemies, pray for them, and return good for evil are exhibiting the character of God himself. Thus they are called "sons of God."

And surely we can realize that there is an inherent happiness which comes with the practice of peacemaking. Is there any happiness in being quick to take offense, eager to find fault and criticize, or anxious to stir up strife? Surely it is a miserable business to be given over to such evil.

Conclusion

Why are there wars being fought in our world? Why is there so much turmoil and strife within our country? Why do so many families experience constant bickering and tension in their homes? Why are so many individuals filled with confusion and despair? All these questions have their answer in a single word: *sin*. The power which has taken peace from planet earth is sin, and the only power which can restore it is the saving power of the blood of Christ.

As much as you might like to have peace with God, peace within your own troubled heart, and peace with people around you, it will remain forever out of your grasp until you repent of your own personal sins and surrender yourself to Christ in obedience to his will. Then, with the experience of peace in your own life, you can share it with others.

Questions for Discussion

1. What are some of the continuing sources of conflict and unrest among human beings?
2. What is the general understanding which people have of the word "peace"?
3. Define the word "peace" as used by Jesus.
4. How is peace established between a person and God? Show that this is necessary to the goal envisioned in this Beatitude.

5. What do you understand by the expression "inner peace"?
6. Discuss the meaning and implications of Philippians 4:7.
7. How does one come to have peace with people around him?
8. What is the place of the church in God's plan to give peace to mankind? Cf. Ephesians 2:13-16.
9. What is the difference between a *tenet of faith* and a *matter of opinion*? Which is usually the basis of contentions among members of the church?
10. What reward comes to a peacemaker?

9/ Happiness is Suffering for Christ

"Blessed are those who are persecuted for righteousness' sake, for theirs is the kingdom of heaven. Blessed are you when men revile you and persecute you and utter all kinds of evil against you falsely on my account. Rejoice and be glad, for your reward is great in heaven, for so men persecuted the prophets who were before you" (Matthew 5:10-12).

Jesus Christ was always completely honest with his disciples. He never promised them a life of ease and luxury in which they would enjoy the esteem of their fellows. Since he was God in the flesh and therefore had supernatural insight about the future, he knew their lives would not be pleasant in this world if they chose to follow his life pattern. So he left no doubt in their minds as to what their fate would be for loyalty to him and his cause on earth.

Whereas other men have sought to entice men to follow them with promises of fame and fortune, Jesus came and enlisted disciples while saying, "The prophets of old are known for their patient endurance of hardships. They suffered at the hands of evil men, because they were seeking the true righteousness which is of God. Now I am inviting you to seek that same righteousness by following me. But I want you to understand that your lot in life will be no easier than that of the prophets about whom you have read. In fact, you will likely have to suffer more intense persecution than they ever experienced. Men will reproach you, persecute you, and say all sorts of evil things about you because of your commitment to me. Now that you know what is in store for those who choose to wear my name, what is your decision?"

As one writer observed, Jesus made it clear that he had not come to make life easy but to make men righteous by passing them through the purifying fires of suffering for his sake.

Any presentation of the gospel to men of modern times which fails to include the plain teaching of Christ about the necessity of suffering for his sake is an incomplete presentation. Jesus did not hide the prospect of suffering from his would-be disciples of the first century. He allowed them to make their decision about discipleship with a full knowledge of what to expect. Men and women today have the same right.

If one decides to become a Christian, he must be prepared to pay the price of consecrated discipleship. Men of previous generations have had to die for their faith in the Lord. Many people today are having to bear the burden of slander, reproach, hatred, and persecution for his sake. But these people have found a happiness in their sufferings which has made it meaningful. Preposterous? Our Savior promised that it would be so.

The Reasons for Persecution

Why should a righteous person have to suffer? Jesus once told the apostles: "Remember the word that I said to you, 'A servant is not greater than his master.' If they persecuted me, they will persecute you" (John 15:20). Jesus certainly did suffer because of his righteous devotion to the will of the Father. Thus we should not think it strange or evil that we should be called upon to suffer while wearing his name.

First, the righteous person will be persecuted because he is different from the world. Jesus' life of radical purity and deep spirituality was a rebuke to the materialistic and hypocritical religious leaders of his day, so they hated him. If a Christian lives the life of consecrated service to the Lord which is demanded by his profession, those around him whose lives do not reflect that standard will resent him. They will attempt to compromise the Christian and bring him down to their level. Failing in such an attempt, they will likely allow their resentment to become hatred and their hatred to generate some form of persecution.

Peter made this same observation when he wrote: "Let the time that is past suffice for doing what the Gentiles like to do, living in licentiousness, passions, drunkenness, revels, carousing, and lawless idolatry. *They are surprised that you do not now join them in the same wild profligacy, and they abuse you*" (1 Peter 4:3-4). These people thought the Christians perfectly "normal" before their conversion. But when they were converted and ceased the practice of sin, the people of the world who had known them previously were "surprised" by them and turned against them. Many a Christian has had this experience upon being converted.

Jesus spoke of this fact in another context and said: "And this is the judgment, that the light has come into the world, and men loved darkness rather than light, because their deeds were evil" (John 3:19). This statement sums up the entire problem in a nutshell. People who are bent on doing evil are not willing to tolerate anything which puts their deeds in true perspective and causes them to be seen for what they really are. Thus men hated Jesus. Thus they hate his faithful followers in every generation.

Just think of the Beatitudes we have studied throughout this series of lessons and how contrary they are to the spirit of the world. Because the traits of character upheld in the Beatitudes are so drastically opposed to the evils of our fellow men, the righteous person who possesses them will certainly arouse the enmity and opposition of those people.

"Poverty in spirit runs counter to human pride; the spirit of mourning concerning one's deficiencies and shortcomings before God is resented by the callous, indifferent, self-satisfied world; a meek and quiet spirit is regarded as cowardly weakness; the craving for righteousness rebukes the cravings of the carnal man; the merciful spirit rebukes the hardheartedness of the world; purity of heart contrasts painfully with the unclean hearts of worldly men; and the peacemakers cannot be endured by the persistently contentious and quarrelsome. Thus do the possessors of righteousness come to be persecuted." [James M. Tolle, *The Beatitudes*, p. 76].

As surely as darkness is opposed to light, evil people of the world will always be opposed to men and women who are intent on the righteousness of God. Thus the righteous will always suffer persecution, because they are different from the world.

Second, the righteous will suffer persecution because of the exclusive nature of true religion. It has always been a rather unpopular thing for men to have religious convictions of any depth. An individual in our own time can hardly make any statement which betrays a conviction on some spiritual matter without being labeled a "bigot" immediately.

The New Testament calls on Christians to be patient and longsuffering with all men (1 Thessalonians 5:14). But it also requires that we be altogether intolerant of false doctrines which compromise the integrity of the gospel message and wicked deeds which compromise its faithful application in the lives of believers (Galatians 1:8-9; 1 Corinthians 5:9-13). In other words, Christians must make a distinction between the sinner and his sins. Toward the sinner's evil deeds we must be uncompromising, while showing love and patience with the sinner himself. No easy task, is it?

Christians of the first century refused to mingle freely

with heathen social life and customs. They refused to enter the temples of the idol-gods of Rome and refused to worship emperors of Rome who demanded worship as "lord and god." Because of this exclusive position, Christians were subjected to suspicion, hatred, and persecution.

Christians of the present day are unpopular when we dare to preach and live the one faith of the New Testament. When we speak of one church, one baptism, and one hope, we become objects of suspicion, hatred, and occasional persecution. If we are bold enough to challenge a doctine or practice that is contrary to the Word of God, a high price may have to be paid. Truth is exclusive and cannot be compromised with error. But just as surely as Christians demonstrate their deep convictions about the truth, they will become targets for those who do not love the truth.

Third, the righteous will suffer persecution when they begin to press the claims of Christ on the unbelieving and wicked world around them. Christians are under obligation to carry the gospel of Christ to the entire creation (Mark 16:15). Many who have that message presented to them will receive it eagerly and gratefully. But there will inevitably be some who react to the same message with antagonism.

Jesus warned the apostles to expect opposition from some because of the message they would be preaching. "If the world hates you, know that it has hated me before it hated you. If you were of the world, the world would love its own; but because you are not of the world, but I chose you out of the world, therefore the world hates you. Remember the word that I said to you, 'A servant is not greater than his master.' If they persecuted me, they will persecute you; if they kept my word, they will keep yours also. But all this they will do to you on my account, because they do not know him who sent me" (John 15:18-21).

There is a war going on between the spiritual forces of Christ and Satan, truth and error, at all times. If any man enlists in the army of Christ and fights the good fight of faith with the sword of the Spirit of God, he surely must expect to suffer at certain times in the course of combat.

A Clarification

Before leaving this matter of the causes which underlie the persecution of righteous people, it should be oberved that some people suffer for reasons other than righteousness.

Jesus did not promise to bless the person who is being persecuted because he is rude, hateful, and unkind in his efforts to tell others about Christ.

Some people appear to have a "martyr complex" and seem to enjoy stirring up animosity toward themselves. When such persons have succeeded in making someone angry through their ill-mannered approach, they leave thinking they have done the Lord's will and will surely be rewarded from on high. That is sheer foolishness. The wild-eyed person who rushes in with apparent self-righteousness to "win a sinner to the Lord" only to drive him completely away from the truth is not the object of the promised blessing in this Beatitude.

It is not the person who brings suffering and persecution upon himself through foolishness and ignorance whom the Lord will bless but the truly dedicated Christian who, in spite of his loving and kind efforts to bring the truth unto others, suffers at their hands because of their wickedness.

The Example of The Savior

The best illustration of the truthfulness of the fact that righteous men will be reviled and persecuted for their righteousness is Jesus Christ. No one was so loving and kind to people as he attempted to bring them enlightenment and salvation. Yet no man was ever so shamefully treated. Many of those who heard the Lord only to be enraged at his teaching said, "He has a demon, and he is mad; why listen to him?" (John 10:20).

Of the abuse he suffered on the day of his death, Matthew gives the following account: "And those who passed by derided him, wagging their heads and saying, 'You who would destroy the temple and build it in three days, save yourself! If you are the Son of God, come down from the cross.' So also the chief priests, with the scribes and elders, mocked him, saying, 'He saved others; he cannot save himself. He is the King of Israel; let him come down now from the cross, and we will believe in him. He trusts in God; let God deliver him, now, if he desires him; for he said, "I am the Son of God." ' And the robbers who were crucified with him also reviled him in the same way" (Matthew 27:39-44).

Ever since the time of Jesus, his faithful followers have been subjected to the same sort of persecution that he endured. Peter and John were brought before the Sanhedrin and threatened with punishment if they continued to preach in the name of Jesus (Acts 4:1-22). Shortly thereafter, all the apostles were brought before this same tribunal and flogged (Acts 5:17-42). Acts 7 tells the story of Stephen who was stoned to death by a mob of unbelieving Jews because of his faith. As a direct outgrowth of the martyrdom of Stephen, the emboldened enemies of Christ began a general persecution of the church at Jerusalem which caused many to have to flee the city for their lives (Acts 8:1).

On and on the story could go of Christians who have had to suffer for their righteousness. The Lord said it would be this way. But he also promised that the patient endurance of such suffering would be rewarded.

Persecution in Modern Times

At this point in our study, someone may be ready to say, "Isn't it a fortunate thing that we live in an enlightened age when persecution because of one's religious convictions is a thing of the past." Now it is true that men are no longer burned at the stake or crucified because of their faith. And I do not know of anyone in jail in the United States because of his righteousness.

What some of us have difficulty realizing is that the

standards of freedom we take for granted in the western world are not universal. There are people in the Soviet Union, South America, China, and other countries of the world who pay a high price for their belief in Jesus Christ. Some are in prison as you read these lines. Even in Western Europe, there are countries where the influence of certain religious groups is so powerful that someone who believes what you do about Jesus and the church cannot get a decent job. Then there are the Islamic countries of the world, where Christian faith is considered a betrayal of race and country. Many people in the world of our day are being persecuted in physical ways for their faith.

Even for those of us who live in the relative freedom of the West, there are persecutions of a subtler nature that many have to endure. After all, Paul said: "Indeed all who desire to live a godly life in Christ Jesus will be persecuted" (2 Timothy 3:12). His statement is not limited by time or circumstances to the first century or two of the church's existence. It is still true today. Persecution may come to us in different ways than it came to Christ, Stephen, and Paul, but it will come to us – if we are living a "godly life in Christ Jesus."

What are some of the forms taken by persecution in our time? I have known of a few people who had to make the decision to become Christians in the light of a clear threat from their families to disown they if they did so. One can be persecuted for righteousness' sake by losing his job because of his religion. For example, some people stand out from others by their refusal to use filthy language or to cheat their employers of honest work they are due to give. Such men may not be tolerated by their non-Christian coworkers who have enough influence to get them fired. One can also be persecuted by having his neighbors avoid him because he is trying to live righteously before God.

One can be persecuted by an unbelieving husband or wife. It is difficult to live a Christian life, attend worship regularly, and rear one's children in the fear of the Lord when all this has to be done against the opposition of a mate.

Or perhaps the Christian involved is a teen-aged girl who refuses to violate the moral purity her Lord demands of her. Her friends – both male and female – may call her a "prude" and cut her off from their social activities. This is suffering for the sake of righteousness.

Maybe a Christian businessman who cannot go along with the dishonest practices of his company will become the object of persecution and lose his position over his convictions. Or perhaps a young man decides to preach the gospel and reveals his intentions, only to be discouraged by his parents who wanted him to enter a lucrative profession or by friends who make fun of him for his "fanaticism" about religion.

No, it simply is not true that persecution for righteousness' sake is a thing of the dim past. Men suffer today for their faith in and obedience to the gospel of Christ. And such suffering is simply a part of the price which every man or woman must be willing to pay in order to be Christ's. Jesus cautioned us to count the cost of discipleship before undertaking its responsibilities. Persecution is part of the cost which each potential disciple will have to take into consideration.

It should also be pointed out that Jesus not only forewarned us about persecution for the sake of righteousness but also *warned about the lack of it.* "Woe to you, when all men speak well of you, for so their fathers did to the false prophets" (Luke 6:26). A person living righteously will face some challenges. So the lack of any persecution is a sort of presumptive evidence against one's complete loyalty to Christ.

Rejoicing in Persecution

Going a bit further, the Lord did more than merely tell his followers to expect and endure persecution. He also commanded, "Rejoice and be glad ..." Be *glad* about being persecuted? What can this mean?

As with everything else in these Beatitudes, the spirit of rejoicing in persecution is diametrically opposite to the spirit of the world. The worldly person cannot imagine any possible reason for rejoicing in the throes of difficulty. The Christian can think of several.

First, he rejoices because he knows that the persecution of the world cannot jeopardize his spiritual security with the Lord. His enemies may take his property, his job, his good name, or even his life. But they cannot take away his citizenship in the kingdom of heaven and the security which comes of such a citizenship. "Blessed are those who are persecuted for righteousness' sake, *for theirs is the kingdom of heaven*" (Matthew 5:10). "And do not fear those who kill the body but cannot kill the soul; rather fear him who can destroy both soul and body in hell" (Matthew 10:28).

Second, he rejoices because his suffering identifies him with God's faithful servants of ages past. As Jesus put it, "Rejoice and be glad ...*for so men persecuted the prophets who were before you*" (Matthew 5:12).

Third, he rejoices because he knows that his suffering will help to create godly fortitude within his spirit. "Count it all joy, my brethren, when you meet various trials, for you know that the testing of your faith produces steadfastness. And let steadfastness have its full effect, that you may be perfect and complete, lacking in nothing" (James 1:2-4).

Fourth, he rejoices because he has a confident hope of heavenly rest after his persecutions on earth have come to an end. "Rejoice and be glad, *for your reward is great in heaven*" (Matthew 5:12a). Paul wrote: "I consider that the sufferings of this present time are not worth comparing with the glory that is to be revealed to us" (Romans 8:18). Keeping your eye fixed on the goal allows you to endure a great deal of pain and unpleasantness while running the race.

Conclusion

Does anyone think Jesus spoke of trials, persecutions, and danger in order to discourage people from following him? Oh, no! Isn't it far more likely that he was not only allowing each of us to know what discipleship would involve by way of difficulty but also hoping to excite us to the thrill and challenge of such a great commitment?

In 1900 Sir Ernest Shackleton, an Arctic explorer, placed an advertisement in the *London Times*. It read: "Men wanted for hazardous journey. Small wages. Bitter cold, long months of complete darkness, constant danger, safe return doubtful. Honor and recognition in case of success." This could be an ad for Christianity. Jesus did not come to offer ease, pleasure, and tranquility. He held out a cross and called for those who would follow him to accept a life of sacrifice. The offer still stands.

Questions for Discussion

1. How realistic was Jesus in preparing his disciples for the consequences of their commitment to him?
2. Why does Christian purity result in suffering for the one who possesses it? Think of an illustration of this from your own experience or from a situation known to you.
3. Discuss 1 Peter 4:3-4 in detail.
4. Discuss the *exclusiveness* of the Christian religion which was referred to in the lesson. How does this produce suffering for a Christian?
5. In what way does evangelism expose a follower of Christ to suffering for righteousness' sake?
6. True discipleship will produce some degree of suffering for every Christian. Does it follow from this that suffering proves a person's religion to be genuine?
7. What are some of the sufferings which early Christians had to endure for the sake of their faith?
8. What types of persecutions are borne by Christians of our generation?
9. What facts make it possible for a Christian to rejoice when he or she is being persecuted?
10. Discuss Romans 8:18 in detail.

10/ Happiness is Heeding Divine Counsel

Jesus announced the secret to true happiness in the Beatitudes. They are statements of the basic attitudes which are necessary for any one of us to be accepted by God and to live the Christian life successfully. Jesus constantly emphasized the truth that *human lives can be happy only when human hearts are right*. And in these Beatitudes are specified the right qualities of heart upon which successful living depends.

It appears to be a universal phenomenon that men believe happiness is dependent on some tangible entity. Happiness tends to be associated with health or the possession of great amounts of money and land. Others tie it to great intellectual attainments or the gratification of sensual desires. It is by these means that we humans have attempted to find happiness and peace of mind. Solomon stands as the best biblical example of the person who sought happiness through these means only to decide that "all was vanity and a striving after wind, and there was nothing to be gained under the sun" (Ecclesiastes 2:11).

Perhaps the great mistake of the human race in this

regard has been our failure to distinguish between *happiness* and *pleasure.* Sin can bring pleasure. The Bible itself says so in Hebrews 11:24-25. "By faith Moses, when he was grown up, refused to be called the son of Pharaoh's daughter, choosing rather to share ill treatment with the people of God than to enjoy the *fleeting pleasures of sin.*" There is no good reason to deny that some sins bring a degree of pleasure. But sin's pleasures are of a momentary and fleeting sort and are far removed from the lasting state of happiness which our Lord is setting before us in the Beatitudes.

Real happiness, as opposed to fleeting pleasure, results from standing in proper relationship to God, men, and self. Only such persons as are poor in spirit, meek, hungry and thirsty for righteousness, merciful, pure in heart, peacemakers, and willing to suffer persecution for the sake of righteousness are living in that blessed state. Thus the study of the Beatitudes is a must for those who would experience the truly happy life.

The Difference Between Christians and Non-Christians

To sum up all that has been said about the Beatitudes and the claims they make on our lives before God, suffice it to say that *they serve to emphasize the difference between a Christian and an unbeliever.* They are a description of the character of Christ. And the more we become like Christ by incorporating these traits into our own character, the more unlike the world we will become.

To say it another way still, the person who begins to study the Beatitudes and comes to desire the character envisioned in them will want to be a Christian. As that person attempts to live the Christian life more perfectly each day, he will find himself adding more of the very virtues which are identified in the Beatitudes.

The Beatitudes are not a collection of rules for the average person. *They are the life goals for the children of God.*

No one can begin to live the sort of life envisioned in the Beatitudes without first surrendering to the Lord's will in becoming a Christian. A man might as well try to win the "Indianapolis 500" without entering the race. A woman might as well try to win a gold medal in the Olympic Games before qualifying as a contestant. You cannot attain the prize of happiness which is set before us in the Beatitudes without first becoming a Christian.

How does one become a Christian? How does he enter the new life which holds such glorious prospects before his eyes?

First, before anyone can legitimately wear the name "Christian," he must believe in the significance and power of the name of Jesus Christ. Acts 4:12 says of this name: "And there is salvation in no one else, for there is no other name under heaven given among men by which we must be saved." This statement was made by the apostles after the Sanhedrin had charged them never to preach again in the name of Jesus Christ. They rejected the charge, because there was no other name by means of which men could be saved. There is no name under heaven like this name. There is no other name in which we can have salvation. The *name* of an individual stands for his very person and all the powers he possesses, and there is no person in all creation who has the power which has been given to Christ alone. He has opened the way to the Father, and no one can come to the Father except by him (cf. John 14:6).

So, before you can be a Christian, you must believe in the special significance of the name of Jesus Christ. You must be made aware of the fact that you can be saved only in obedience to his will as stated in the New Testament.

Second, before you can wear the name of Christ, you must not only believe in it but also be baptized into it. In 1 Corinthians 1:12-13, in the course of his argument against the divisive party spirit at Corinth, Paul deplored the fact that men were calling themselves after other human beings. "What I mean is that each one of you says, 'I belong to Paul,' or 'I belong to Apollos,' or 'I belong to Cephas,' or 'I belong to Christ.' Is Christ divided? Was Paul crucified for you? Or were you baptized in the name of Paul?"

From these verses, please observe the two requirements that must be met before any person has the right to wear another's name in religion: (1) that person has to have been crucified for you, and (2) you have to be baptized into the name of that person. Paul's argument was to the effect that no one at Corinth could wear his name or Peter's or Apollos' because none of them had died for the sins of people at Corinth and none of them had baptized the Corinthians into their names. In making his negative argument, however, he let us know quite clearly that no person has the right to wear Christ's name until he has been *baptized into that name.*

A woman is not a Christian simply because she lives in America; a man is not a Christian because he holds membership in some religious organization. There is more involved. There are requirements which have been established by divine authority. One must believe in Christ as the Son of God and accept the fact that salvation is available only in his name. Then he must be baptized into Christ – baptized for the remission of sins (Acts 2:38) and into such a relationship with Christ that he can wear his name henceforth.

Entering the Kingdom of Heaven

You have probably noticed that Jesus spoke of the "kingdom of heaven" in these Beatitudes. In fact, the first and last Beatitudes promise the same reward – "for theirs is the kingdom of heaven." The Savior began and ended these sayings by emphasizing that one who possesses these traits belongs to a different kingdom than people of the world. Those who lack these spiritual qualities are still in the kingdom of Satan, darkness, and sin. Those who have added these traits to their lives are in the kingdom of God, light, and righteousness.

The kingdom of God is the rule of God in the hearts and lives of his people. And while the terms "church" and "kingdom of God" are not precisely coextensive (e.g., both babies and angels are in the kingdom but are not members of the church), the kingdom business of God in this world is being done through the church.

The church was purchased unto God through the blood of Jesus (Acts 20:28), is the "one body" of Christ (Ephesians 4:4; cf. Colossians 1:18), and is Christ's holy bride (Ephesians 5:21-33). Such radical changes are involved in becoming a part of the kingdom of God on earth that Jesus compared it to being born anew. "Truly, truly, I say to you," Jesus told the Jewish ruler Nicodemus, "unless one is born anew, he cannot see the kingdom of God" (John 3:3). In other words, just as we became members of our human families by means of a fleshly birth, so we become members of the family of God by experiencing a new, spiritual birth.

Jesus went on to explain to Nicodemus that the new birth involves two elements – water and Spirit. "Truly, truly, I say to you, unless one is born of water and the Spirit, he cannot enter the kingdom of God" (John 3:5). The only ordinance of the Christian religion that involves water is baptism, yet the power of baptism is not in water but in the quickening power of the Spirit of God. When an individual obeys Christ in the act of baptism, the blood of Christ cleanses him of all sin and allows him to rise from that watery grave to a new life in Jesus (Romans 6:4).

Living in Newness of Life

For someone to come into a saving relationship with Christ is for Satan to suffer defeat. And he does not take defeat with good cheer. "Your adversary the devil prowls around like a roaring lion, seeking someone to devour" (1 Peter 5:8). He will not give up on the person who has come to Christ for salvation and happiness. He will do his best to bring him back under condemnation. For that reason, we need to be alert to his tactics and firm in our determination to resist him.

For one thing, Satan will tempt each of us where he or she is weakest and most vulnerable. Simon of Samaria was a vain man who wanted others to hold him in esteem as "some great one." When he was converted to Christ, the devil immediately set about to overthrow him through an appeal to that weakness. Seeing the apostles work miracles and impart the gifts of the Holy Spirit to men, Simon thought how wonderful it would be to have their power. He was led of Satan to offer to buy the power the apostles had (Acts 8:9-24). His pride and desire for the limelight got the best of him. His inordinate desire for acclaim and greatness was his weakness, and it was there Satan tempted him.

This is the way the tempter works still. He will attempt to take away newfound happiness in Christ by appealing to the old weaknesses. Lustful and sensual people will be tempted by people, scenes, and situations designed to draw them into immorality. People with bad tempers will be tempted to impatience. Satan will watch for times when you are especially liable because of stress, depression, or urgent need. When you are in the throes of crisis, he will offer you an "easy way out" via sin.

For another, Satan will try to appeal for a new convert to abandon the new life for the old one recently left behind through old friends and companions in evil. Your former associates in sin will laugh at the "puritanism" in your new life; they will label you "Holy Joe" or "Holy Jane" and chide you for "thinking you are better" than they are. Anyone who becomes a Christian needs to expect this sort of pressure and have his mind made up as to how to react to it. Will you give up Christ to hold onto sinful friends? Will you be willing to forfeit their favor in order to follow Christ? Jesus said some people would have to give up family and friends in order to follow him (Mark 10:29-30).

Also, babes in Christ need to realize that conversion has not destroyed the desires for old sins and their accustomed pleasures. There will still be "flashbacks" of desire to taste the pleasures of sin.

This is why a commitment to newness of life must involve a healthy fear of sin and a firm determination to resist it. The person who has found the blessedness of release from sin can find himself caught again in Satan's trap, if he does not keep himself from situations which are likely to involve temptation. For example, many an alcoholic has gone for years without a drink. Then he took just one drink at an office party – and the vicious cycle began all over again. It is never safe for a person whose weakness is for alcohol to put himself in contact with it again. The same principle applies to any and all sin. You must never expose yourself willingly to a situation where you will be pressured to take just "one little taste" of some sinful pleasure. Don't see that person again with whom some past immorality was shared – no matter what pretense of necessity Satan may suggest. Don't pick up one of those magazines again or even walk to the rack where they are. Don't go to a party where alcohol is going to be served.

Finally, let your commitment to newness of life show itself in the very positive ways of involvement in the life of the local church, formation of Christian friendships, service to others in the name of Christ, daily prayer and study of the Word of God. Fill your life with the things that will draw you closer to Christ and every good thing associated with his work in this world.

Conclusion

What is the conclusion to this series of meditations on the Beatitudes? It is stated very simply: *Happiness is Heeding Divine Counsel.*

If you want the true, deep, and lasting happiness which only God can give, then follow the specific teachings of the Word of God. Heed divine counsel about becoming and living as a child of God. Walk in newness of life, with a firm resolve to resist Satan's attempts to draw you back into sinful and forbidden paths.

You will be at peace with God, for in becoming a child of God your sins are washed away (Acts 22:16) and through daily faithfulness to Christ are kept away through continual cleansing by the blood of Jesus (1 John 1:7). You will be at peace with all other men and women who are also children of God, for they are your brothers and sisters in

Christ. And you will be at peace with yourself, for heeding divine counsel gives one a clear conscience before Almighty God (1 Peter 3:21b).

Now that you have had an opportunity to glimpse the character envisioned in the Beatitudes and the happiness which attends it, surely you will want to devote the remainder of your days to the development of these traits in your personality. Or, to state it more correctly, I hope you will yield yourself to God so he can begin his divine work of building these qualities into your personality as he transforms you into the likeness of the Son.

Questions for Discussion

1. Is there a distinction between "pleasure" and "happiness"? Explain your answer.
2. Can one know the blessedness envisioned in the Beatitudes apart from being a child of God?
3. How does one become a Christian?
4. Discuss the implications of 1 Corinthians 1:12. Can one be a Christian who has not been baptized by Jesus' authority?
5. What is the "kingdom of heaven"? What is its relationship to the church?
6. Can one be saved apart from the body of Christ?
7. According to John 3:1-5, what must take place in order for one to enter the kingdom of heaven? Explain the new birth.
8. What will be the attitude of Satan toward anyone who embraces the new life in Christ?
9. What are some of the things Satan uses to draw people back into sin?
10. What benefit has come to you from a study of the Beatitudes?